THE PLEASURES AT YOUR SIDE

THE PLEASURES AT YOUR SIDE

Papers from the Wanaparthy Samasthan

1832–1911

Edited by
BENJAMIN B. COHEN

Orient BlackSwan

THE PLEASURES AT YOUR SIDE: PAPERS FROM THE WANAPARTHY SAMASTHAN, 1832–1911

ORIENT BLACKSWAN PRIVATE LIMITED

Registered Office
3-6-752 Himayatnagar, Hyderabad 500 029, Telangana, India
e-mail: centraloffice@orientblackswan.com

Other Offices
Bengaluru, Chennai, Guwahati, Hyderabad, Kolkata, Mumbai, New Delhi, Noida, Patna

First published by Orient Blackswan Private Limited 2019
Reprinted 2022

ISBN 978-93-5287-696-9

Map cartographed by
Sangam Books (An imprint of The Agricultural Development Commercial Credit And Industrial Investment Company Private Limited)

041571

Typeset in
Constantia 10.5/12.6
by Le Studio Graphique, Gurgaon

Printed in India at
Avantika Printers Private Limited, New Delhi 110 020

Published by
Orient Blackswan Private Limited
3-6-752, Himayatnagar, Hyderabad 500 029, Telangana, India
e-mail: info@orientblackswan.com

For Raja Rameshwar Rao III

(1923–1998)

Contents

Map 

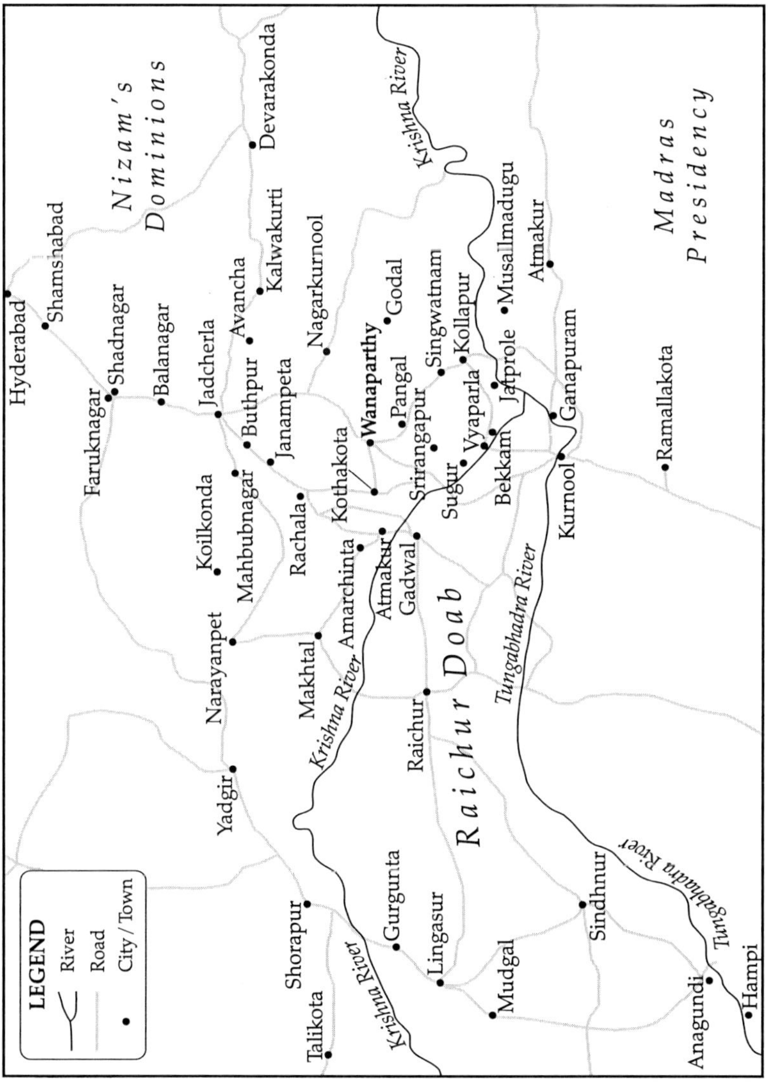

Nizam's Dominions
Madras Presidency
Raichur Doab
Krishna River
Tungabhadra River
Hyderabad
Shamshabad
Shadnagar
Faruknagar
Balanagar
Jadcherla
Koilkonda
Mahbubnagar
Buthpur
Avancha
Kalwakurti
Devarakonda
Janampeta
Nagarkurnool
Rachala
Kothakota
Wanaparthy
Godal
Pangal
Srirangapur
Singwatnam
Kollapur
Vyaparla
Sugur
Bekkam
Jatprole
Musallmadugu
Atmakur
Ganapuram
Kurnool
Ramallakota
Amarchinta
Gadwal
Narayanpet
Makhtal
Raichur
Yadgir
Shorapur
Talikota
Gurgunta
Lingasur
Mudgal
Sindhnur
Anagundi
Hampi

LEGEND
River
Road
City / Town

Glossary 

abwab	Taxpayers; the tax imposed.
anna	The sixteenth part of anything, but most often of a rupee.
Bahadur	Honorific title, literally 'valiant'.
bahiri	Eagle.
Balwant	Honorific title; literally 'full of might'.
bega	A measure of land. In the Deccan, under the Adil Shahi Dynasty, a *bega* was just less than an acre.
chaukidar	An official in charge of a *chauki*; a watchman.
deshmukh	Hereditary officer exercising police and/or revenue authority over a district.
deshpande	Hereditary revenue accountant of a district.
fatwa	A judicial decree; judgement; sentence.
faujdar	Army officer; an officer responsible for police and having jurisdiction over criminal matters; a criminal judge; a magistrate.
ghat	A landing place; quay; wharf; ferry; bathing-place.
havaldar	A chief of a company of guards; a police officer; a commander of a fort.
hundi; hundikar	A bill of exchange; one who holds or writes such bills.
ilaqa	A property; an estate.
inam	Land held rent-free, usually perpetually and hereditarily; a reserved portion of assessable revenue; grants of rent-free land.

jagir	A land tenure in which public revenues were made over to a servant of the state.
jagirdar	One who holds a *jagir.*
jama kamil	Final standard assessment.
jamedar	A leader or chief of any number of persons; military subaltern; an officer of police or customs.
jatra	A fair.
jawan	Soldier or police officer.
jowar	Sorghum.
kani	One quarter of a sixteenth; 1/64.
katta	A measure equivalent to five *seer*s.
khas	Select; special; also private, peculiar.
khilat	Robe of honour; usually presented with a title or appointment.
Kulkarni	A title associated with accountants, record keepers or tax collectors.
kulthi	A combination of lentils and leafy vegetables.
masha	A unit of mass, now standardised as .97 grams.
man-o-pan	Honorary rights or privileges that come with official rank.
maniwar; maniwari	District revenue accountant; superintendent of police. The right to hold such position.
mansab; mansabdar	A hereditary title; one who holds a *mansab*.
mashaikh	Muslim legal scholar.
maund	A unit of measurement; the south Indian *maund* was fixed at 25 pounds.
mohur; mohur ashrafi	Gold coin; a gold coin issued by dynasties valued at two *mohur*s.
naib	A deputy; representative; lieutenant.
nar'gaur; nar'gauri	Head of shepherds as holding a claim on revenue of a village or district; head revenue and police officer of a district (similar to a *deshmukh*); the right to

claim this position. (Likely a form of the Marathi term *nadgir* or *nargun*.)

naru — A type of tumour.
Nazim-e-jamiat — Irregular army department.
nazrana — Gift; tribute; payment, especially from an inferior to a superior.
paisa — A copper coin valued at four to the *anna*, and 64 to the rupee.
pala — A unit of weight.
panchayat — A council; a village council; a caste council.
pandan — A box for holding betel and accoutrements.
pargana — A subdivision of a district; province; tract.
patti — Part of a *taluq*.
peshkash — An offer; payment.
pujari — Priest
risaladar — Officer commanding a troop of irregular horses.
rusum — Customary fees; perquisites; customary payments and gratuities.
ryot — A subject, a cultivator; a peasant labourer.
samasthan — Hereditary noble or chief; area ruled by such a family.
sanad — Royal letter; decree; contract.
sarbasta — A grant less than *peshkash*; land given on a contract basis.
sarkar — The state; government; supreme authority.
saudagar — A merchant; a trader.
Sawai — Honorific title, literally 'a quarter better than other people'.
seer — A unit of weight or liquid measure equal to about one kilogram or one litre; a fortieth of a *maund*.
sibandi — Irregular soldiery or police.
subah — A province; a large subdivision.
takiddar — A messenger sent to give an injunction or warning.
taluq — A subdivision of a district.

taluqdar	A magistrate or revenue officer over a district or part of a district.
tehsil	Collection; revenue collected from land; revenue from a group of villages.
tehsildar	Chief revenue and police officer of a division of a district (*taluq*); an officer subordinate to the *taluqdar*.
than	A cloth measuring 16 yards.
tola	A weight of 12 *masha*s.
vakil	Agent; intermediary between rulers; attorney.
wasul baqi	Collection and application. The administration of the revenues.
watan; watandar	Country; residence or native place; home. One who holds or occupies such a location.
zamin	Land; earth; ground.
zamindar	A landholder.
zat jagir	Assignment of land for personal support.
zila	District; land subdivision.
ziladar	A district or portion thereof holder.

Introduction

Seventy-five miles southwest of Hyderabad city is the town of Wanaparthy. During the Asaf Jahi period, when Hyderabad city served as the capital of His Exalted Highness the Nizam's Dominions (also known as Hyderabad State), Wanaparthy was the capital of a *samasthan* by the same name. A samasthan was a geographically contiguous domain with a hereditary royal head or chief, the raja or sometimes maharaja. The Wanaparthy samasthan occupied a location at the periphery of Hyderabad State's geography—it bordered the Tungabhadra River, which in turn was the southern border of the Nizam's Dominions, separating it from the Madras Presidency. Wanaparthy and the other samasthans within Hyderabad State were generally peripheral to the daily workings of the Nizam's Government in Hyderabad, yet they played an important role in the state as the oldest members of its political composition.

This collection of papers from Wanaparthy illuminates the relationship between the urban centre of Hyderabad and the peripheral country capital of Wanaparthy.[1] While we know a great

[1]Thanks to Chandra Mallampalli, Munis Faruqui and Choon Hwee Koh for their comments and linguistic expertise. For a history of the samasthans in Hyderabad State, see Benjamin B. Cohen, *Kingship and Colonialism in India's Deccan: 1850–1948* (New York: Palgrave Macmillan, 2006). Three brief histories of the Wanaparthy samasthan exist in Telugu: Rachayata Krishna, *Wanaparthi Samasthana Charitra* (Kurnool: Hyderabad Printers, 1948); Namatari Venkat Shastri, *Wanaparthi Samasthan Charitra* (Hyderabad: Orient Longman, 1992); A. Mohan Reddy, *Wanaparthi Samasthan Telugu Sahityaseva* (Hyderabad: Orient Longman, 1998). The samasthans of both Hyderabad and Andhra territories have been examined from a literary angle in Acharya Tumati Donappa, *Andhra Samasthamulu Sahitya Poshammu* (Hyderabad: Pravardana Publications, 1969). For some

deal about the Nizams, their Prime Ministers and some political participants in the urban centre of the state, this collection provides an unprecedented view of the daily workings within the samasthan. The documents offer a glimpse into how the leaders of Wanaparthy organised their domain, replete with armed forces and revenue collection, how the Nizam's Dominions organised its supporters, and how the two centres of power functioned within the larger colonial context of nineteenth-century India. While much scholarship has centred on nobles of the capital or the equivalent colonial official (the British Resident), these documents take us into the countryside and the inner workings of a 'little kingdom'.[2]

Within the Nizam's Dominions, the samasthans were a unique group. There were fourteen in all: Gadwal, Wanaparthy, Jatprole, Amarchinta, Paloncha, Gopalpet, Anagundi, Gurgunta, Narayanpet, Domakonda, Rajapet, Dubbak, Papanapet and Sirnapalli.[3] Ruling families of different caste backgrounds (Reddys, Velamas, etc.) governed the samasthans, and power passed by succession from father to son or, sometimes, from husband to wife. Occasionally, families adopted an heir from a distant branch of its genealogical tree. Most samasthans had origins dating to the Kakatiya era, thus they were the oldest members of Hyderabad's political milieu.[4] By the early

---

further accounts of the samasthans, see Raman Raj Saksenah, *Qadim Dakani Saltanaten Aur Samastan* (Hyderabad: Husami Book Depot, 1996). On Hyderabad's political system in the nineteenth century, see Karen Leonard, 'The Hyderabad Political System and Its Participants', *Journal of Asian Studies* 30, no. 3 (1971), pp. 569–82.

[2] On the idea of 'little kings' and some examples, see Bernard Cohn, 'Political Systems in Eighteenth Century India: The Banaras Region,' *Journal of the American Oriental Society* 82, no. 3 (1962), pp. 312–20; Nicholas B. Dirks, *The Hollow Crown* (Cambridge: Cambridge University Press, 1987); Pamela Price, *Kingship and Political Practice in Colonial India* (New York: Cambridge University Press, 1996).

[3] Shorapur is also sometimes included in this list.

[4] There are innumerable histories of different Deccan empires. For the Kakatiyas, see Cynthia Talbot, *Precolonial India in Practice: Society, Religion, and Identity in Medieval Andhra* (Oxford: Oxford University Press, 2001). For Vijayanagar, see Burton Stein, *Vijayanagara* (Cambridge:

twentieth century, these domains comprised about 10 per cent of Hyderabad's total land and an equivalent percentage of the state's population, that is, about 1.5 million people. Wanaparthy was the second largest in terms of both revenue and prestige.[5]

Cities, towns and villages mentioned in this collection are scattered throughout an area, from Hyderabad city in the north to the banks of the Krishna in the south. This area near the river was Palamoor District, but in 1890, it was renamed as Mahbubnagar in honour of the sixth Nizam, Mahbub Ali Khan. It is now part of the state of Telangana. The region had a wide variety of flora and fauna, critical to the largely agricultural economy of Wanaparthy. Land brought under cultivation produced grains (*jowar, bajra,* rice, etc.) as well as cotton, and some fruit including grapes and mangoes. Wanaparthy and the surrounding areas remain famous for mangoes and, as we shall see, this precious fruit finds mention in the collection (for example, No. 275). Low jungle vegetation and some dense forests marked the region's uncultivated land. This variety of habitats provided for a wide array of animals, both domestic and wild. Domesticated animals included water buffalo, cows, pigs, goats and other species common to the subcontinent. More interesting, both to nobles who called the Deccan home and to visitors from far afield, was the array of wildlife that made

---

Cambridge University Press, 1993); Phillip Wagoner, '"Sultan among Hindu Kings": Dress, Titles and the Islamicization of Hindu Culture at Vijayanagara', *The Journal of Asian Studies* 55, no. 4 (1996), pp. 851–80. On Golconda see John Richards, *Mughal Administration in Golconda* (Oxford: Clarendon Press, 1975); Abdul Majeed Siddiqui, *History of Golconda* (Hyderabad: The Literary Publications, 1956). Also useful is Susan Bayly, *Saints, Goddesses and Kings: Muslims and Christians in South Indian Society, 1700–1900* (Cambridge: Cambridge University Press, 1989). For a single-volume colonial account of the Deccan, see J.D.B. Gribble, *A History of the Deccan*, first published 1896 edn, 2 vols, vol. 1 (New Delhi: Rupa & Co., 2002).

[5] The Wanaparthy samasthan occupied about 450 square miles, with a population of nearly 63,000. It had an annual income of Rs 1.5 lakh, and it paid an annual fixed tribute of Rs 76,883 to the Nizam's Government coffers. Mirza Mehdy Khan, *Imperial Gazetteer of India Provincial Series Hyderabad State*, Reprint 1991, Atlantic Publishers, New Delhi edn (Calcutta: Superintendent of Government Printing, 1909).

for excellent hunting. Tigers, leopards, bison, deer, antelope and other game were common. Other fauna included wild hog, bears, partridge, quail and duck.

Under foot, the land yielded valuable minerals, especially in the area near Wanaparthy. Samasthan families and other local lords mined diamonds, gold and coal on both sides of the Krishna.[6] The Tungabhadra, a feeder river, enlarges the Krishna about 20 miles south of Wanaparthy town. As the Krishna flowed eastwards, it formed the southern boundary of the Nizam's Dominions, and the districts of Mahbubnagar, Nalgonda and Warangal. The river, when met by the Tungabhadra, formed the boundaries of the Raichur *doab* (two waters). The doab was under the control of Hyderabad, with intermittent control shifting to the British. Caught in this flux was the Gadwal samasthan, located in the doab just west of the confluence of the two rivers.[7]

The Nizam's Dominions in 1901 had a population of 11,141,142. Hyderabad city, the most populous urban centre in the state, had a population of 448,466.[8] Beyond the city, population density rapidly decreased. The area around Wanaparthy had only fifty-four people per square mile, compared with more densely populated areas such as Bidar, Medak and Gulbarga, where densities reached 184 persons per square mile. Of the population, 46 per cent were Telugu speakers, 26 per cent spoke Marathi, 14 per cent spoke Kanarese and 10 per cent spoke Urdu or Hindustani. The dominant religion of the Nizam's Dominions was Hinduism, with 88 per cent of the population, while followers of Islam comprised the second-largest group with 10 per cent. Christians, Jains, Sikhs, Parsis and animists formed the remaining 2 per cent.

[6] One account of diamond mining in the area comes from 'A Description of the Diamond-Mines as It Was Presented by the Right Honourable, the Earl of Marlbal of England to the R. Society', *Philosophical Transactions* XII (1677), pp. 907–16.

[7] P.M. Joshi, 'The Raichur Doab in Deccan History—Re-Interpretation of a Struggle', *Journal of Indian History* 36, no. 3 (1958), pp. 379–96.

[8] Khan, *Imperial Gazetteer*, p. 20.

Deccan Empires

The Wanaparthy samasthan's history dates to the Kakatiya Kingdom of Warangal (11th–14th c.). When it collapsed under repeated attacks from northern invaders in the thirteenth century, members of its court and military establishment faded into the countryside.[9] These individuals, now operating in a temporary power vacuum, carved out territories in the Deccan and established themselves as independent rulers. By the sixteenth century, the Vijayanagar Empire (14th–16th c.), with its capital at Hampi, had taken shape, and many of these local rulers found security and employment in the service of the Vijayanagar rulers. Yet, others sided with the Bahmanis (14th–16th c.) and later the Qutb Shahis of Golconda (16th–17th c.). Alliances did not necessarily form along religious lines. The samasthan rulers and their armies fought with and against the sultans of the Bahmani and Qutb Shahi empires. Most notable were several Hindu rulers who fought with their northern Muslim neighbours against Ramaraya of Vijayanagar when they met at Talikota in 1565.[10] These individuals provided military support to campaigns waged by larger regimes of the day.[11] When called upon, they attended court ceremonies and received honours (titles, land,

[9] On the larger political situation, see Richard M. Eaton and Phillip B. Wagoner, *Power, Memory, Architecture: Contested Sites on India's Deccan Plateau, 1300–1600* (New Delhi: Oxford University Press, 2014).

[10] Rulers of the Gadwal samasthan, located in the eastern Raichur doab are one example of this; IOL (India Office Library, London) R/1/1/1469, Foreign and Political Department. Later, during the early Mughal administration of Golconda, the heads of the Jatprole samasthan readily sought employment and boons from their new masters at Hyderabad; Richards, *Mughal Administration*.

[11] Clearly, notions of a sixteenth-century 'clash of civilisations' must be rewritten. This is in reference to Samuel Huntington's popular work of the same name: Samuel Huntington, *The Clash of Civilizations and the Remaking of World Order* (London: Penguin, 1996). This idea of a civilisational clash has been read backwards into history by members of India's historical, political and literary circles. For a summary of this, see William Dalrymple, 'India: The War over History', *New York Review of Books*, 7 April 2005.

revenue entitlements). In their own country capitals, they began to take on royal trappings, often replicating what they had seen at the imperial capitals.

Hyderabad city and state were built upon the remnants of Golconda, which itself was built upon the remains of empires that preceded it. Such has been the pattern throughout much of South Asia's history of dynasties, empires and imperial powers. The Golconda and Asaf Jahi regimes incorporated the samasthans into their framework, providing a political superstructure into which they fitted different polities. In 1589, then sultan of Golconda, Muhammad Quli Qutb Shah, laid out plans for a new city a few miles away from the overcrowded fort of Golconda. The epicentre of this new city would be the Char Minar, which still serves as the most-recognised symbol of Hyderabad. The quartered city grew and prospered with its trade in precious stones, refined culture and ample opportunities. However, in 1687, Mughal Emperor Aurangzeb laid siege to the fort while his troops ransacked the city. Through treachery, the Mughal forces finally overcame the mighty doors of Golconda; the Qutb Shahi regime was all but over. In its place, Aurangzeb appointed Asaf Jah I, the family name of the Nizams.

The period covered in this collection includes the reign of the last four Nizams. The fourth Nizam, Nasir-ud-Daula, took office in 1829. For the first part of his tenure, Prime Minister Raja Chandu Lal guided him until the latter's resignation in 1843. The Nizam reigned during a time of fiscal difficulty for his state. By the middle of the century, payment for the British-backed Hyderabad military contingent had fallen behind and, under pressure, the Nizam ceded the northern districts of the state, the Berar, to the British as payment. After Chandu Lal, came Siraj-ul-Mulk, and Hyderabad's most famous Prime Minister, Salar Jung, followed him.[12]

[12] On the life of this esteemed Prime Minister, see Cheragh Ali, *Hyderabad (Deccan) under Sir Salar Jung*, vol. 1 (Bombay: Education Society's Press, 1885); Vasant Kumar Bawa, *Hyderabad under Salar Jung I* (New Delhi: S. Chand & Company Ltd., 1996).

In May 1857, as storm clouds gathered in the Bengal Presidency, Nizam Nasir-ud-Daula died. His son Afzal-ud-Daula succeeded him as the fifth Nizam. During the events of 1857, the Nizam sided with the British, who rewarded him for his loyalty in the years that followed. For instance, in addition to a monetary reward of £10,000, Lord Canning awarded him in 1861 the Most Exalted Order of the Star of India with a class of Knight Grand Commander, GCSI.

When Afzal-ud-Daula died in 1869, his infant son Mahbub Ali Khan was a toddler of only three years. Under the Regency of Salar Jung and Nawab Shams-ul-Umra, with a watchful eye cast by the British Resident, the young Nizam was groomed for leadership. Mahbub Ali Khan, as the sixth Nizam, was installed in 1884, with a full retinue of Hyderabad's nobles present for the occasion (including the samasthan rajas, see Nos 322–28) as well as British dignitaries including the Resident and Lord Ripon.

Administrative changes brought about by Salar Jung marked the first two decades of the Nizam's life. The Prime Minister recruited north Indians and created numerous departments to help streamline the state's aging administrative structure. Some of these included police, revenue and judicial departments as well as reforms in the state's currency, mints and transportation. Once Mahbub Ali Khan received full ruling rights, he continued on a path of reform, albeit not at the same pace as Salar Jung. Twice the Nizam attended the Delhi durbars, and he would have attended the third (held in the winter 1911), but he died before the event.[13] Mahbub Ali Khan was in some respects the first 'modern' leader of the state, well versed in the culture and politics of colonial India, yet retaining much of Hyderabad's refined culture. His son, the seventh and last Nizam of Hyderabad, Osman Ali Khan, does not figure much in this collection other than it was he, and not his father, who attended the 1911 durbar along with members of the Wanaparthy samasthan.

Serving under the Nizams was an expansive order of nobles, military men and bureaucrats. At each level of the political

[13] Narendra Luther, *Hyderabad: A Biography* (New Delhi: Oxford University Press, 2006), pp. 166–78.

hierarchy, individuals expressed loyalty and performed service to those above them while commanding obedience and a similar loyalty from those beneath.[14] Directly below the Nizam's family in the hierarchy were the Paigah nobles and beneath them were the samasthan families as well as the elite ministers of the time—men like Raja Rameshwar Rao of Wanaparthy as well as Maharaja Kishen Pershad—both of whom figure heavily in this collection. Beneath this level were large landowners, high-ranking administrators and members of the legal system. Still further down in the political chain were smaller landowners, government officials and businessmen. Finally, near the bottom were soldiers, craftsmen and petty government officials. Many of these individuals find their voices in this collection as they petition the Wanaparthy family for favours, financial assistance or other matters.

Wanaparthy, till 1832

The early rulers of Wanaparthy samasthan followed a pattern of service under different Deccan rulers. The samasthan maintained almost complete autonomy throughout, and it served others by the choice of its leaders, not by compulsion or force. While the Wanaparthy family traces its history back to the court of Warangal, the historical record becomes somewhat clearer by the early sixteenth century (c. 1510). At this time, an individual named Veer Krishna Reddy established himself at the village of Patapalli, a few miles north of the Krishna River.

This was the first of several capitals for the family. By the end of the century, the family shifted to Sugur (Soogoor), and then to Kotha Kota ('new fort') around 1686. In some references, the samasthan is known by the name Sugur. By the eighteenth century, the family shifted again to Srirangapur (possibly under the leadership of Raja Venkat Reddy in 1727), where the family

[14] A schematic of Hyderabad's social system during the time of Mahbub Ali Khan can be found in Harriet Ronken Lynton and Mohini Rajan, *Days of the Beloved* (Berkeley: University of California Press, 1974). See the graphic between p. xiii and p. 1.

deity is worshipped, and finally to Wanaparthy town in 1807, which remained the capital until 1949.[15] Both Sugur and Kotha Kota find frequent mention in the letters of the collection, as they remained important military and trade centres in the area.

Several generations of able leaders succeeded Veer Krishna Reddy during which time the samasthan grew in strength. By the mid-seventeenth century, the service that the samasthan provided to the rulers of Golconda warranted recognition. Then ruler *ashta basha* (eight language) Gopal Rao (r. 1657–1675) received the title of *bahiri* (eagle) from the house of Golconda—a title used by all the subsequent (male) rulers of the samasthan. Gopal Rao's wife, Janaki (also referred to as Janamma, r. 1686–1691) succeeded him and served as Regent during the childhood of the young Kumara Bahiri Gopal Rao. Under Janaki's leadership, the Nizam called on the Wanaparthy ruler to help maintain law and order in the area. Of immediate concern was Surabhi Narayan Rao of Jatprole, who had rebelled and was subsequently brought to justice, in part, by Janaki and her forces.[16] Again, several generations pass before we come to Raja Ram Krishna Rao (1789–1820). Seeking to increase both his ceremonial and real power, the Raja made several requests to the Asaf Jahi house. First, he requested the honorary title of *bahadur* (valiant), which he received, and this remained a hereditary title within the family. Second, he requested a larger collection of armed forces to be paid in part from the revenue formally sent to Hyderabad. These new troops included nearly 250 *sawar*s (troops) and one elephant.[17] Finally, Ram Krishna Rao requested and received permission to mint Wanaparthy coins at the Sugur mint. Only four samasthans within the Nizam's Dominions enjoyed such a privilege: Gadwal, Wanaparthy, Shorapur and Narayanpet.

---

[15] K. Krishnaswamy Mudiraj, *Pictorial Hyderabad,* 2 vols, vol. 2 (Hyderabad: Chandrakanth Press, 1934). p. 622.

[16] Qutb Shah to Janaki, 21 May 1687, WFP (Wanaparthy Family Papers, Hyderabad.). For a history of Jatprole, see V. Sadasiva Sastrulu, *Sri Surabhivari Vamsa Charitramu* (Madras: Saradamba Vilasa Press, 1913).

[17] Confirmation of this request came in a letter: Sikandar Jah to Ramkrishna Rao, 11 December 1817, WFP.

Just two years before the first documents of this collection begin, we have an eyewitness account of the Wanaparthy samasthan and its neighbours. This account comes from the intrepid traveller Enugula Veeraswamy. Veeraswamy was a Niyogi Brahman born in Madras around 1780. Having studied English, Tamil, Telugu and Sanskrit, he joined the East India Company as an interpreter and rose to the position of 'Head Interpreter' of the Madras Supreme Court. In May 1830, he embarked on a pilgrimage to Benares (Kashi *yatra*) and, along the way, kept a journal in Telugu of his travels and impressions. Having crossed the Krishna River from the Madras Presidency into the Nizam's Dominions, Veeraswamy found himself in the Wanaparthy and Jatprole samasthan territory. Unfortunately, at the time, the two samasthan families were in some sort of dispute. These petty intrastate disputes were common and, according to Veeraswamy, provided much grist for political manipulation by Hyderabad officials.

> There are several Zamindars under the Nawab of Hyderabad as in the case of Venkatagiri and Kalahasti. This village is a part of the estate of the Zamindar of Kolhapuram [Jatprole]. These Zamindars pay limited tributes to the Nizam and enjoy autocratic powers in their estates. The stronger Zamindars, it is said, do not pay even this tribute regularly. At such times, the Hyderabad Government pursues them and succeeds in extracting its tribute by force. When these Zamindars disagree with each other they not only fight each other to death but also raid each other's villages and cause havoc tormenting the ryots and ravaging the villages. When such tussles arise, Diwan Chandulal and his followers delight in further aggravating such situations being conscious of the resultant money profit to them. A tussle of this kind is going on between the Zamindar of Vanaparthi and Zamindar of Kolhapuram at the time of my travel.[18]

Veeraswamy's first-hand account of the two samasthans shines light on their complex relationship to the Nizam's of Hyderabad.

[18] Enugula Veeraswamy, *Enugula Veeraswamy's Journal (Kasiyatra Charitra)*, trans. P. Sitapati (Hyderabad: Andhra Pradesh Government Oriental Manuscripts Library & Research Institute, 1973). p. 19.

At times, Hyderabad officials largely ignored the samasthan families except to collect their annual tribute. At other times, Hyderabad officials participated in or interfered with the running of the samasthans. Finally, a third type of interaction occurred whereby the relationship between Hyderabad officials and the samasthan rulers was particularly close. Clearly, at the moment Veeraswamy passed through Wanaparthy, neither relations between Wanaparthy and Jatprole were particularly good nor was the relationship with Hyderabad.[19]

Wanaparthy, 1832 to 1857

The first documents in the collection date from 1832. At this time, the Nizam was Nasir-ud-Daula, aided by his Prime Minister, Raja Chandu Lal. Across the Musi River at the British Residency, Josiah Steward served as Resident. At Wanaparthy, the samasthan was under the able leadership of its Rani. Wanaparthy and several other samasthans (Gadwal, Jatprole and Gopalpet) all enjoyed the tenures of women leaders. Three years later in 1835, at the age of fourteen, Raja Rameshwar Rao I assumed charge of the Wanaparthy samasthan.

Rameshwar Rao led the samasthan through the events of 1857 and for nearly a decade afterwards, until his death in 1866.[20] His tenure as head of the samasthan is characterised by an elaborate dance between loyalty to both the Asaf Jahi house and the British, and the immediate needs at home. On the former side, Rameshwar Rao was repeatedly promoted within the Nizam's state forces. He held the positions of Brigadier of the State's Forces, Inspector General of the Cavalry and Inspector General of the Nizam's field forces. Further, he received the hereditary title of *balwant* (full of might) from the Asaf Jahis. A more tangible marker of his own charisma and power was his ever-increasing armed retinue. These forces included soldiers

[19] Even more difficult to assess due to the paucity of records is the fate of the ryots and everyday inhabitants of Wanaparthy.

[20] A biography of Rameshwar Rao exists in Telugu: *Sri Raja Prathama Rameshwara Rayalu* (Hyderabad: Orient Longman, 1990).

of African descent, thus giving the Wanaparthy forces a distinct look when they marched in battle or came to Hyderabad city.[21]

On the domestic front, Rameshwar Rao came under the influence of events and cultural practices from across the river in the Madras Presidency. For instance, he had his own samasthan surveyed and settled, following the standards used in the Madras Presidency. This survey bears the name of its major author, Anantharam Chitha, and was completed in 1855. Further, Rameshwar Rao married a woman named Shankaramma. Having no children, he married her younger sister, Janamma, to whom he gave the name Catherine. He sent Janamma to Madras where she received an education in a Presbyterian school, and he made her wear frocks and English dresses as well.[22] Not fully satisfied with her cultural exposure, Rameshwar Rao brought her brothers into the samasthan family, giving each names more familiar to British history than Indian: Henry, William, Charles, James and Edward.

Rameshwar Rao also demonstrated a mischievous penchant, which on more than one occasion placed him at the receiving end of Asaf Jahi and British displeasure. In April of 1855, the Resident at Hyderabad (George Bushby) summoned the Raja to Hyderabad to face charges for robbery, unlawful seizure of the Gopalpet samasthan and circulating debased coinage. This was a time of rampant rumours and speculation about what exactly Rameshwar Rao might or might not have done. The correspondent from the *Englishman* put it bluntly, 'Everything here is so distorted that every question has two sides to it, of an almost equal balance, and there is no speculating upon results.'[23] By summer's end, the Raja was convicted and sentenced to four years' imprisonment. However, sentencing at this time was lenient, and it is unclear if he faced anything as difficult as house arrest.[24]

---

[21] Shanti Sadiq Ali, *The African Dispersal in the Deccan* (Hyderabad: Orient Longman, 1995). pp. 196–97.

[22] Lynton and Rajan, *Days of the Beloved*, p. 181.

[23] *Englishman* in *Hyderabad Affairs,* vol. IV, 19 April 1855.

[24] *Englishman* in *Hyderabad Affairs,* vol. IV, 11 August 1855.

1857

When the events of 1857 began to unfold, Rameshwar Rao reaffirmed his loyalties to the Asaf Jahis and the British in two ways. First, he penned a letter to the Governor General, The Viscount Canning, offering his services to put down the 'barbarous and atrocious' conduct of the 'mutineers'.

> With the deepest anxiety and horror have I heard and read of the barbarous and atrocious conduct of the Mutineers of the Bengal Presidency, and their coldblooded and deliberate proceedings are of such a nature, as to stamp them with imfamy [*sic*], and brutality, unknown in the Histories of the most savage and uncivilized nations. Hence my sympathies towards the British have been roused [*sic*], and my wrath against the rebels has been kindled, so that if the offer herein made is accepted, I am resolved to avenge the atrocities committed on the subjects of the Crown of England, with an unsparing hand.[25]

While his offer was ultimately refused, likely due to fears of unsteady or disloyal forces, the offer itself won the Raja a good deal of thanks and praise from British officials.

Before a final decision concerning Rameshwar Rao's offer to fight the 'mutineers', the then Resident Cuthbert Davidson added his own candid opinion.

> The Rajah has been at Hyderabad for some months and has been most anxious to make himself useful to me. He has had to a certain extent an English education, and he is, I feel certain, loyal and sincere in his offers. He is much respected by his own people, who are of a predatory and warlike class, he would have no difficulty at any time in collecting around him a considerable body of armed followers, ready to do his bidding in any way, although I imagine he considerably over-estimates his powers when he talks of a complete Brigade of Cavalry Infantry and guns, as he has no means of paying and supporting them.[26]

[25] Rameshwar Rao to GOI, 12 September 1857, NAI (National Archives of India, New Delhi), Foreign Department.

[26] Cuthbert Davidson to Fort William, 14 September 1857, NAI, Foreign Department.

Finally, in a letter to Rameshwar Rao from G.F. Edmonstone, Secretary to the Government of India, he writes:

> I have received and laid before the Right Hon'ble the Governor-General in Council your letter to the address of His Lordship, dated the 12th ultimo, praying to be allowed to render the British Government some Military aid in quelling the present insurrection in its Dominions. In reply I am desired to acquaint you that His Lordship in Council feels assured that Your Highness' troops would, if called into the field, do excellent service. But the re-taking of Delhi, and the arrangements that have been made for punishing the mutineers in all other directions renders it unnecessary for the Government to accept the aid of your troops. The Governor-General in Council desires me, however, to express to you the thanks of the Government for your offer, and its approbation of your feelings of loyalty and attachment towards it.[27]

The Government of India rewarded Rameshwar Rao's loyalty in the post-1857 years. In February 1862, he received a double-barrelled rifle, a sword, a sword belt and a pair of matching revolvers.[28]

A second event cemented his loyalty to the British. To the north and west of Wanaparthy, the young Raja of Shorapur, Venkattapa Naik, chose to fight Company forces.[29] Shorapur itself was considered a samasthan, and thus Rameshwar Rao's offer was likely seen as a positive counter-example to the actions of Naik. This connection to Shorapur appears in the collection. Documents Nos 129 and 132 both refer to Rameshwar Rao's movement towards Shorapur territory to help secure the area. Ultimately, Rao was involved in the capture of young Naik.

[27] Edmonstone to Rameshwar Rao, 21 October 1857, NAI, Foreign Department.

[28] Davidson to Rameshwar Rao, 28 February 1862, WFP.

[29] For an account of Shorapur in the mid-nineteenth century, see Philip Meadows Taylor, ed., *The Story of My Life*, AES Reprint 1986 edn (New Delhi: Asian Educational Services, 1882).

Wanaparthy, 1857 to 1911

After Rameshwar Rao's death, his wife Rani Shankar Amma administered the samasthan as Regent. Upon the adoption and succession of young Raja Ram Krishna Rao III, Richard Temple—the Resident at Hyderabad in 1867–1868—addressed Rani Shankar Amma. 'I now congratulate you on your son's succession. I hope he will imitate the example of loyalty and fidelity set by the late Rajah. And I trust that Wonpurthy territory may always enjoy the advantage of the good system of management which has been established in it.'[30] Tragically, Ram Krishna Rao died in a riding accident, and Rani Shankar Amma adopted a young heir named Rameshwar Rao II. He was sent to the Madras Christian College for his education. During the time of Rameshwar Rao II, the Nizam's Government constructed a railway line that passed near Wanaparthy town, but not directly through it. Legend says that the family did not wish to have the Nizam or his officials 'dropping in' on them. Such visits would require elaborate arrangements and the customary payment of *nazr* (tribute). Under Rameshwar Rao II's tenure, he received the title of 'Maharaja' (great king), and secured for his two sons the title of 'Raja'. These two sons were Ram Krishna Rao and Ram Dev Rao. When the Raja died, neither son was old enough to assume control and the Nizam's Government temporarily placed the samasthan under the jurisdiction of the Court of Wards.[31] Again, tragedy struck as the older Ram Krishna Rao died unexpectedly, leaving behind his widow and infant son, Rameshwar Rao III. After some litigation, the path was clear for Rameshwar Rao III to assume the *gaddi* (throne) and lead the samasthan in the last years of its existence.

In its final years, Wanaparthy samasthan had for its neighbours the Gopalpet samasthan (also a blood relative to the rulers of Wanaparthy) to the northeast and the Jatprole samasthan to the southeast. Across the river to the south was the

[30] Richard Temple to Rani Shankar Amma. 3 January 1867, WFP.

[31] On the role of the Court of Wards and the samasthans of Hyderabad State, see: Benjamin B. Cohen, "The Court of Wards in a Princely State: Bank Robber or Babysitter?," *Modern Asian Studies* 41, no. 2 (2007).

larger and powerful Gadwal samasthan, and to the immediate north, different *jagir* and *dewani* lands bounded Wanaparthy.

In 1948, during the tumultuous year after India's Independence, Rameshwar Rao III crafted a document of accession for the samasthan to directly join the Indian Union. This act not only demonstrated his commitment to the new democratic India but also rested on a belief that the samasthan had always believed itself sovereign in some way, even if paying *peshkash* (tribute) to the Asaf Jahis. Rameshwar Rao gave the document to Jayaprakash Narayan who delivered it to Sardar Patel.[32] However, it was never needed as Prime Minister Nehru ordered a 'police action' that brought the Nizam's Dominions into the folds of the new Indian republic.[33]

The Wanaparthy samasthan was officially transferred to the interim Hyderabad Government on 15 September 1949. As the last Raja of Wanaparthy, Rameshwar Rao III handed over to General J.N. Chaudhuri the keys to the samasthan treasury. He asked members of the samasthan administration to cooperate fully with the General and the new interim Hyderabad Government. We can assume that within the palace the collection of papers herein, in some form or other, lay waiting.

The Collection

The collection spans nearly a century from the first decades of the nineteenth century to the imperial climax realised at the Delhi durbar in the winter of 1911–1912. It contains three broad categories of correspondence. First, there are letters *from* the Wanaparthy samasthan rulers to officials at Hyderabad (the Nizam, the Prime Minister, the Majlis, etc.). Second, there are letters *to* the samasthan rulers from not only Hyderabad officials but also a variety of individuals who served the samasthan in some way. Petitions and letters come from impoverished individuals,

---

[32] Nehru Memorial Library, New Delhi; Tape No. 4454, Rameshwar Rao III.

[33] For essays on these events, see: Omar Khalidi, ed. *Hyderabad: After the Fall* (Wichita: Hyderabad Historical Society, 1988).

soldiers, and patrons of the family, each requesting some form of support. Finally, the collection contains correspondence between other parties that in some way concerns the samasthan, so a copy was sent to the Wanaparthy palace. In modern parlance, the samasthan family was 'cc'd' or carbon-copied on these correspondences.

In addition to the voices of the Wanaparthy samasthan rulers, in particular Raja Rameshwar Rao I, the collection contains correspondence from other well-known Hyderabad officials. At the top of the political order was the Nizam who personally signed a few letters. While the Nizams hosted the different Wanaparthy rulers on many occasions, the correspondence within the collection is less personal and more logistical in nature. For instance, in No. 129 dated 10 February 1858, the Nizam grants Raja Rameshwar Rao increased powers along the border with the Shorapur samasthan. At another time, an order, No. 309 dated 12 May 1872, from the Nizam to then Raja Ram Krishna Rao, orders those along his path to the Balaji *jatra* (a fair) to provide him with necessary provisions, and also requests British officials to allow the Raja to travel with arms through British territory, 'should the need arise'.

While correspondence from the Nizam is perfunctory in nature, a flurry of letters to the Nizam surrounding the coronation of Mahbub Ali Khan in 1884 is more revealing. As the new ruler of the Asaf Jahi house was about to take power, it was an opportune time to voice one's concerns and reinforce one's rank within the political hierarchy. At this time, young Raja Rameshwar Rao II ruled at Wanaparthy, and through his *vakil* (agent), Seshgir Rao, he seemed particularly interested that both he and other members of neighbouring samasthans be invited to the coronation and behave in an appropriate way (Nos 322 and 327).

More common than letters to or from the Nizam are those to or from the Prime Ministers of Hyderabad. This is not surprising as it was the role of the prime minister to handle the day-to-day business of the state. Central to the concerns of officials was the prevalence of crime within the Nizam's Dominions, and the Prime Minister's office frequently sent descriptions to the samasthan officials of criminals thought to be entering Wanaparthy territory. No. 12 dated 29 June 1835, from Chandu Lal, is one such letter describing Udayya, presumably wanted for some crime or another. Other correspondence is more reflective of the cooperation and communal goodwill between Hyderabad officials and their countryside counterparts, in contradiction to the impression given by Enugula Veeraswamy. For instance, in No. 14 dated 5 March 1846, the Prime Minister grants permanent funds for the eternal lamp of a temple at Amriyakal within Wanaparthy territory.

Woven throughout the correspondence are references to the other major power broker in the Nizam's Dominions—the Resident. Although few letters of the Resident appear in this collection, the Residents knew the rulers of Wanaparthy, and their correspondences are found elsewhere. Within this collection, the Resident largely appears as a figure to whom one should not cause offence. Again, criminals were particularly worrisome to Hyderabad officials, and the Nizam's officers—to add weight to their own orders—frequently invoked the Resident. For instance, No. 38 of 12 September 1846 alludes to letters from both Raja Ram Baksh (Prime Minister) and the Resident (James Stuart Fraser) concerning a criminal, Narasimha Reddi, who, along with 250 Rohillas, the samasthan forces were to apprehend. In another instance, the needs of British forces in the region are expressed and passed along down the political hierarchy ending with the Wanaparthy rulers. In February 1850, a large body of troops departed Mysore en route to Secunderabad. Mysore officials contacted the Residency at Hyderabad, who in turn passed orders to the Prime Minister, who finally passed them along to Rameshwar Rao stating that he should provide supplies to the troops when they passed through Wanaparthy territory (No. 59). This order, like many others, ends with a stern warning to make sure that 'no complaint of any kind in this regard comes to the Government'. Besides the Residency, the Wanaparthy family made use of other British resources, for instance, No. 84 of 4 October 1854 shows how the Raja sought out Western doctors for medical attention.

In addition to the Nizams, Prime Ministers and Residents, the rulers of the Wanaparthy samasthan had contact with and demonstrated an awareness of their fellow samasthan rulers. Wanaparthy shared borders with Jatprole, Gopalpet and, across the river, Gadwal. Each of these makes some appearance in the collection. At Jatprole, the rulers of that samasthan appeared to have both skirmished with the Wanaparthy family as well as occasionally angered Hyderabad officials. In a letter to Sir Salar Jung from Rameshwar Rao, No. 91 of 2 January 1855, the Raja recounts his engagement with the ruler of Jatprole. The latter seems to have confined him and brought him to Hyderabad to face punishment. The Gopalpet samasthan also appears within the collection, but unlike the skirmishes with Jatprole, the rulers of Gopalpet and Wanaparthy at one time shared a common bloodline. For instance, in No. 88 of 24 December 1854, attempts by Rameshwar Rao to reclaim revenue from Gopalpet were thwarted as the latter samasthan had been taken over by the Hyderabad Government. However, the Gopalpet samasthan's revenue was eventually returned to the Wanaparthy house, as is evident in Nos 307 and 308 of 1871–72. The matter seemed all but over, but No. 339 of 15 February 1887 and No. 340 of January/February 1887 suggest that claims over the Gopalpet samasthan's revenues remained contested. The correspondence coming from Wanaparthy maintains that due to the original agreement and the subsequent violation of that agreement by the Gopalpet house, that samasthan should revert to Wanaparthy control. Finally, while the Gadwal samasthan finds brief mention in other correspondence, it is in the last document that the relationship between the Gadwal and Wanaparthy samasthans becomes clear. For the Delhi durbar of 1911, the Raja of Gadwal, Sita Rambhupal II, was unable to attend the event (he was a minor under the supervision of the Court of Wards), but he gave a small gratuity to the Wanaparthy contingent that appears in the receipt for the event (No. 343).

Other entries in the collection reveal a wide array of social, political, economic and other insights. No. 15 of 1838–39 shows the ways in which the samasthan rulers and the agriculturalists who served them at times fell into distress and devised forms of relief. Similarly, entries such as No. 20 of 26 November 1840 reveal the value placed on agricultural products like guavas and pomegranates, now ubiquitous, which were mentioned in an exchange between elites. Later, mangoes sent from Wanaparthy to Hyderabad had the 'sweetness of sugar' (No. 275 of 1870–71). Entries like No. 68 of 6 August 1851 show the role of the samasthan rulers in clearing land, establishing agricultural fields, and developing wells and tank irrigation. Water problems appear again in No. 190 of 19 November 1860 when villagers obstructed a stream. Law and order were a constant concern for the samasthan rulers, the Nizams and British authorities. Entries like No. 21 of 1840–41 and No. 38 both refer to the 'troublesome' Rohillas, while No. 57 highlights the role of horse rustling. Later, 'mischievous' Rohillas and Arabs alike are to be detained so as not to give trouble to passing British troops (No. 248 of 1868–69). Moneylenders emerge as a community with considerable influence, for example, in No. 36 of 1846—not finding the Wanaparthy Raja accommodating, they approached officials in Hyderabad for redress. Arabs also acted as moneylenders, but they became a problem when they harassed debtors as shown in No. 67 of 25 March 1851. New technology began to appear in Hyderabad and in the samasthans during the mid-nineteenth century. For instance, No. 224 of 9 October 1868 refers to 'electric poles', while No. 238 of 1868–69 mentions that engineers were being sent to the area to survey land for the 'steam carriage', i.e., the railway. The Wanaparthy family faced some pressure to invest in the railway, as seen in No. 272 of 24 January 1870.

Provenance

The provenance of the collection is itself important. Leading the effort to have the papers translated and published was Rameshwar Rao III. After turning over the samasthan to the interim Hyderabad Government, he went on to serve under Prime Minister Jawaharlal Nehru in the Foreign Service as First Secretary in the Indian Commission in Nairobi. He was elected five times (1957, 1962, 1967, 1971 and 1977) as a Member of Parliament to the Lok Sabha from Mahbubnagar District where Wanaparthy town is. Rameshwar Rao III gave the palace at Wanaparthy for use as a college, and we can assume that the papers found a new home with him in Hyderabad city. In the 1980s, he began to have the collection translated.

The original collection consisted of Persian, Urdu, English and some Telugu papers. These documents were generally 4 to 8 inches wide and varied from a few inches to over a foot in length. At the top of the documents, a seal usually marked the sender's identity. The letters were handwritten on high-quality paper. At a later date, the originals were photocopied. In this process—likely an attempt to preserve the originals—the tops and bottoms of the documents occasionally failed to be copied, thus obscuring the seal and identity of the sender as well as the date. In some cases, we can recover the sender's identity through context, while in others we are left only guessing.

Throughout the 1980s, different hands worked to translate the collection. Various numbering systems appear in the upper corners of the individual documents, but none is particularly consistent. The photocopy of the original document was attached to a typewritten English translation. English language editors checked and corrected for clarity, and raised questions about specific points of translation. Different initials appear on the documents as translators and editors worked on them. On some translations, it is clear what the proper translation should be, while on others, it remains left open to interpretation.

Some documents from the collection have been omitted. There are several reasons for this. First, in some cases, documents are of a similar style and function. For instance, No. 18 is a simple receipt and record of payment for horseman Mir Fasahat Ali. The collection contains over 100 such similar receipts, thus one has been included to serve as an example of the many. Second, some documents contain neither date nor any reference to a datable event or person, and thus were omitted. Finally, a few documents were unintelligible in their translation, often further marred by having no date. Those that had only a datable year are placed at the end of each year's documents. For those who wish to delve deeper into the collection, Rameshwar Rao III donated the original papers to the Andhra Pradesh (now Telangana) State Archive, Tarnaka, Hyderabad.

Finally, most editors have the luxury of seeing a project through, from start to finish, of knowing the contributors and of working with those involved in the technical aspects (especially translation) of a project's development. Unfortunately, I have enjoyed none of these luxuries. This collection emerged as a book project nearly two decades ago, long before I became involved. Its progenitors and journeymen are sadly gone now, and thus I have not benefited from a direct understanding of their intentions. Several translators worked on different parts of the entire collection, but they too are gone, and it has been my immense task to interpret their English renderings of Indian language prose. In many cases, I felt it best to leave their interpretations untouched. For instance, 'the pleasures at your side' might be understood as, 'your well-being'—a phrase used elsewhere in the collection, but the original seems more in the spirit both of poetic nineteenth-century prose and the translators' own lovely rendering. In addition, I have left in place the translators' different English renderings of personal names, thus for example, 'Narsiah' rather than the more common 'Narsaiah'. The early English translations of the collection had a superabundance of terms in Persian, Urdu or Telugu. This made the manuscript difficult reading, thus where an English term could be substituted, I have made that translation. Also, place names, wherever possible, have had their spellings standardised.

Unlike editors who can take full responsibility for a collection, in this case, I can claim only a share of the responsibility: my share being both more complicated by the collection and its own history, yet eased somewhat by the many others that have come before me who have helped to make this collection possible. To them, no amount of gratitude would suffice.

March 2019 BENJAMIN B. COHEN
Salt Lake City, Utah, US

References

Ali, Cheragh. 1885. *Hyderabad (Deccan) under Sir Salar Jung*, vol. 1. Bombay: Education Society's Press.

Ali, Shanti Sadiq. 1995. *The African Dispersal in the Deccan*. Hyderabad: Orient Longman, 1995.

Bawa, Vasant Kumar. 1996. *Hyderabad under Salar Jung I*. New Delhi: S. Chand & Company Ltd.

Bayly, Susan. 1989. *Saints, Goddesses and Kings: Muslims and Christians in South Indian Society, 1700–1900*. Cambridge: Cambridge University Press.

Cohen, Benjamin B. 2007. 'The Court of Wards in a Princely State: Bank Robber or Babysitter?' *Modern Asian Studies* 41, no. 2: 395–420.

———. 2006. *Kingship and Colonialism in India's Deccan: 1850–1948*. New York: Palgrave Macmillan.

Cohn, Bernard. 1962. 'Political Systems in Eighteenth Century India: The Banaras Region', *Journal of the American Oriental Society* 82, no. 3: 312–19.

Dalrymple, William. 2005. 'India: The War over History', *New York Review of Books*, 7 April, pp. 62–65.

'A Description of the Diamond-Mines as It Was Presented by the Right Honourable, the Earl of Marlbal of England to the R. Society', *Philosophical Transactions* XII (1677): 907–16.

Dirks, Nicholas B. 1987. *The Hollow Crown*. Cambridge: Cambridge University Press.

Donappa, Acharya Tumati. 1969. *Andhra Samasthamulu Sahitya Poshammu*. Hyderabad: Pravardana Publications.

Eaton, Richard M., and Phillip B. Wagoner. 2014. *Power, Memory, Architecture: Contested Sites on India's Deccan Plateau, 1300–1600*. New Delhi: Oxford University Press.

Gribble, J.D.B. 2002. *A History of the Deccan*. First published 1896 edn, 2 vols, vol. 1. New Delhi: Rupa & Co.

Huntington, Samuel. 1996. *The Clash of Civilizations and the Remaking of World Order*. London: Penguin.

Joshi, P.M. 1958. 'The Raichur Doab in Deccan History—Re-Interpretation of a Struggle', *Journal of Indian History* 36, no. 3: 379–96.

Khalidi, Omar, ed. 1988. *Hyderabad: After the Fall*. Wichita: Hyderabad Historical Society.

Khan, Mirza Mehdy. 1909. *Imperial Gazetteer of India Provincial Series Hyderabad State*. Reprint 1991 Atlantic Publishers, New Delhi edn. Calcutta: Superintendent of Government Printing.

Krishna, Rachayata. 1948. *Wanaparthi Samasthana Charitra*. Kurnool: Hyderabad Printers.

Leonard, Karen. 'The Hyderabad Political System and Its Participants', *Journal of Asian Studies* 30, no. 3 (1971): 569–82.

Luther, Narendra. 2006. *Hyderabad: A Biography*. New Delhi: Oxford University Press.

Lynton, Harriet Ronken, and Mohini Rajan. 1974. *Days of the Beloved*. Berkeley: University of California Press.

Mudiraj, K. Krishnaswamy. 1934. *Pictorial Hyderabad*, 2 vols, vol. 2. Hyderabad: Chandrakanth Press.

Price, Pamela. 1996. *Kingship and Political Practice in Colonial India*. New York: Cambridge University Press.

Reddy, A. Mohan. 1998. *Wanaparthi Samasthan Telugu Sahityaseva*. Hyderabad: Orient Longman.

Richards, John. 1975. *Mughal Administration in Golconda*. Oxford: Clarendon Press.

Saksenah, Raman Raj. 1996. *Qadim Dakani Saltanaten Aur Samastan*. Hyderabad: Husami Book Depot.

Sastrulu, V. Sadasiva. 1913. *Sri Surabhivari Vamsa Charitramu*. Madras: Saradamba Vilasa Press.

Shastri, Namatari Venkat. 1992. *Wanaparthi Samasthan Charitra*. Hyderabad: Orient Longman.

Siddiqui, Abdul Majeed. 1956. *History of Golconda*. Hyderabad: The Literary Publications.

Sri Raja Prathama Rameshwara Rayalu. 1990. Hyderabad: Orient Longman.

Stein, Burton. 1993. *Vijayanagara*. Cambridge: Cambridge University Press.

Talbot, Cynthia. 2001. *Precolonial India in Practice: Society, Religion, and Identity in Medieval Andhra*. Oxford: Oxford University Press.

Taylor, Philip Meadows, ed. 1882. *The Story of My Life*. AES Reprint 1986 edn. New Delhi: Asian Educational Services.

Veeraswamy, Enugula. 1973. *Enugula Veeraswamy's Journal (Kasiyatra Charitra)*, trans. by P. Sitapati. Hyderabad: Andhra Pradesh Government Oriental Manuscripts Library & Research Institute.

Wagoner, Phillip. 1996. '"Sultan among Hindu Kings": Dress, Titles and the Islamicization of Hindu Culture at Vijayanagara', *The Journal of Asian Studies* 55, no. 4: 851–80.

1832

No. 1
1832–33

List of articles (jewels and clothes) gifted to Raja Rameshwar Rao, his two mothers, his stepmother, and to his *vakil*, sent through Mirza Muhsin.

Jewelled tools, two pairs.
Gold headgear ornament, one.
Necklaces, six.
Tassel, one.
Jewelled waist band, two pairs.
Clothes, six sets.
Ornamented shawls, one pair.
Brocade, six *than*s.
Nanded silk, two *than*s.
Nanded turban, one.
Banaras saris with blouses, two (one yellow and one red).
Earrings, two pairs.

No. 2
1832–33

Gracious Raja Sahib

I have not received a single *paisa* of my salary for three years starting from 1830–31. All that I received is a letter containing some remarks and excuses. But there is no point in making such poor excuses. This would only cause displeasure and hurt a long-standing friendship.

You can imagine my plight under these circumstances. The butcher and the baker are here, and you may question them in connection with this matter. You may also cross-examine the *naib* of Amrabad to verify the amount.

My salary for a year amounts to Rs 2,400, and for three years it comes to Rs 7,200. Kindly verify this and issue orders for the payment of my salary.

ꙮ

No. 3
1832–33

Gracious Sri Sawai Raja Rameshwar Rao Bahiri Balwant Deshmukh *pargana* Sugur, etc.

From your friend, Siva Ram, blessings.

All is well here. Write about the pleasures at your side Pertaining to the salaries of Syed Khasim, horsemen, etc., for the year 1831–32, it is noticed that the aforesaid *jamedar* was paid an amount of Rs 400 in excess. The said *jamedar* is a poor man. Therefore, it is written. The excess amount paid to him may be recorded in four instalments at Rs 100 per annum for four years, instead of deducting it in a lump sum from the payment for the year 1832–33. In this way not only will the excess payment be recovered easily but also the aforesaid *jamedar* will be saved from hardship. The said *jamedar* is one of the important persons to you. That is all.

1833

No. 4
3 October 1833

Gracious Sri Bhavani Das Samstuka Rao Esq.

Friend: Rachala Hanmantha Rao, resident of Wanaparthy.

All is well here. Write about the pleasures at your side. As per the word put by gracious Sri Sawai Raja Rameshwar Bahadur to Mir Abdul Hadi, an amount of only Rs 625 has been received by us. In this connection, the receipt was submitted to you. As such, the amount may be paid on the very next day after the completion of 47 days. After a total of 47 days, the receipt may be taken back after the amount is fully paid up.

ஐ

No. 5
1833–34

Gracious Sri Sawai Raja Rameshwar Rao Bahiri Balwant Bahadur Deshmukh *pargana* Sugur, etc. From your friend, Rai Rachur Laxma Raidu, blessings.

All is well here. Write about the pleasures at your side. The salary of Sri Sesha Rao Muthasaddi Sugur has been deducted in the estimates for the years 1832–33 and 1833–34, for which a mutual assignment till the end of the year 1832–33 was made. However, the payment even to that extent was stopped. Now the year 1833–34 has elapsed. Not a single coin has been paid so far. Therefore, he complained to His Excellency. Now we have received the orders about Rai Bahadur, so we are writing. We do not understand how the salary for two years has been put under confusion. What would be the consequence of shouts like these from paid servants? Do they consider it to be proper to be heard at the higher level? You are wise enough, and you know better. No worry. So it is written. Now the peon Bhale Sahib has come. As soon as you receive this letter, the salary for the years 1832–33 and 1833–34 may be paid in full without any further delay. Be it known to you.

ஐ

No. 6
1833–34

Gracious Sri Sawai Raja Rameshwar Rao Bahiri Balwant Bahadur Deshmukh *pargana* Sugur, etc. From your friend, Shyama Raidu, blessings.

All is well here. Write about the pleasures at your side. It has come to be known that the salary of Muhammad Taqi Khan *jamedar* for the year 1833–34 has not been paid so far. Therefore, it is being written. His Excellency has accorded the sanction for the payment of the *jamedar*. As such the salary may be paid to him without any delay. See that no objections are raised with the payment. The case in this regard should not be allowed to reach this level. That is all.

ꕤ

No. 7
1833–34

Gracious Sri Sawai Raja Rameshwar Rao Bahiri Balwant Bahadur Deshmukh *pargana* Sugur, etc. From your friend, Siva Ram Pandit, blessings.

All is well here. Write about the pleasures at your side. You have paid the salary of Mir Azeem Ali Ustad for the year 1832–33 to Mir Bahaddur Ali Suke Mir. Now for the current year, i.e., 1833–34, the salary of the Mir is being included in the estimate while creating a provision for his post. So it is informed. Now the expenditure on him has become a troublesome state of affair. He is the Ustad to [illegible]. The salary that is due to him may be paid in full immediately as per the estimate by obtaining the necessary acquittance. He is an elderly person. Without evading for more days, the payment may be made soon. The case in this regard should not be allowed to reach this level.

ꕤ

No. 8
1833–34

Gracious Sri Sawai Raja Rameshwar Rao Bahiri Balwant Bahadur Deshmukh *pargana* Sugur, etc. From your friend, Siva Ram Pandit, blessings.

All is well here. Write about the pleasures at your side. The salaries of Dewlath Khan and other Government servants, horsemen for the year 1833–34 are included in the estimate. The same may be paid in accordance with the estimate without fail. The previously mentioned Khan is regularly present in the Government. So it is written. He may be paid without making any delay and sent back. That is all.

No. 9
1833–34

Gracious Sri Sawai Raja Rameshwar Rao Bahiri Balwant Bahadur Deshmukh *pargana* Sugur, etc. From your friend, Siva Ram Pandit, blessings.

All is well here. Write about the pleasures at your side. The salaries of Muhammad Taqi Khan and other commanders for the current year, i.e., 1833–34 was included in the estimate as per the orders of His Excellency. Therefore, it is written. Hence, the salary of the said Khan may be paid in accordance with the estimate in full. Until then, the daily expenses may be paid to the horsemen. The complaint in this regard should not be allowed to reach this level. That is all.

No. 10
1834–35

Gracious Sri Sawai Raja Rameshwar Rao Bahiri Balwant Deshmukh *pargana* Sugur, etc.

From your friend, Shyama Raidu, blessings.

All is well here. Write about the pleasures at your side. The salaries of Ishwarji, the courier, pertaining to the year 1834–35 are included in the estimate as per usual practice. Therefore, it is informed. He has come to you with the order and the list of instalments. Hence, his pay in lump sum may be paid as per the list, after obtaining his signature on the roll.

He has to be always present before the gracious Raja Sahib. Therefore, his payment may be made as early as possible. See that the case in this regard may not come to this level in the future.

ꝏ

No. 11
1834–35

To Raja Ram Baksh Bahadur

Gracious Sri Sawai Raja Rameshwar Rao Bahiri Balwant Bahadur Deshmukh *pargana* Sugur, etc.

From your friend, Shyama Raidu, blessings.

All is well here. Write about the pleasures at your side. The salaries of Syed Ahmad Ali Khan and others for the year 1834–35 have been included in the estimate. Therefore, Khan has come to you with the orders issued from Sreemanth (His Excellency the Nizam). So it is being written. The salary of Khan may be paid in full in accordance with the estimate. The complaint about this should not be allowed to reach to this level.

No. 12
29 June 1835

Seal

Rajayan-e-Raja, Raja Chandu Lal Maharaja Bahadur

Udayya, son of Naganna, caste Chetty Lingam is a resident of Yellareddipalle. His complexion is pale brown. He has a broad forehead, thick bushy eyebrows and black eyes. There is a scar from a wound made by a stone on his right eyebrow. Another scar of the same kind is on the left side of his forehead. There are marks of cowpox on his face. He has also got pierced ears.

1836

No. 13
5 March 1836

Shri Rameshwar Swami

Seal

Rajayan-e-Raja Maharaja Chandu Lal Bahadur,
servant of the Aristotle of the time,
the Rustum of the era, Nizam-ul-Daulah,
Muzaffar-ul-Mumalik,
Nizam-ul-Mulk, Asaf Jah.

To the present and future revenue collectors of *pargana* Sugur and Kothakota, *sarkar* Pangal, *subah* Farkhunda Bunyad, Hyderabad.

They are hereby informed that Rs 50 has been sanctioned for the monthly salaries and expenses of the *pujaris*, including stationery. In accordance with the Government orders, the road on the bank of the Krishna River will be opened from 19 March 1836. This road has been agreed upon as compensation to the above-mentioned *pargana*. Therefore, the salary, in consultation with Raja Sawai Rameshwar Rao Bahadur, may be disbursed to the *pujaris* every month. An accurate disbursement register prepared according to the Government pro forma must be maintained by the aforesaid Raja. Secondly, the above-mentioned amount must be adjusted in the account book of the above-cited *pargana* according to this *sanad*.

ຽ

No. 14
5 March 1836

Seal

Rajayan-e-Raja Maharaja Chandu Lal Bahadur,
servant of the Aristotle of the time,
the Rustum of the era, Nizam-ul-Daulah,
Muzaffar-ul-Mumalik,
Nizam-ul-Mulk, Asaf Jah.

This is written to the present and future revenue collectors of *pargana* Sugur, *sarkar* Pangal, *subah* Farkhunda Bunyad, Hyderabad.

An amount of eight *annas* per day has been sanctioned for the expenses of the eternal lamp of the temple located in Amriyakal village in the above-cited *pargana* from 19 March 1836 as compensation for the above-mentioned *pargana* and *sarkar*. Therefore, the said amount must be paid daily without keeping back any arrears, after deducting the difference between solar and lunar days, for the expenses of the temple. An accurate disbursement register must be maintained in accordance with the Government pro forma. Secondly, according to this document, after the above amount is paid, it must be noted and adjusted in the account book of the above-cited *pargana*.

1837–1838

No. 15
1838–39

Order under the seal of Raja Yar-e-Raja Maharaja Chandu Lal Bahadur.

[Signed]

Order in the name of Raja Bal Krishna Reddi, *deshmukh* of *pargana* Amarchinta and *pargana* Waddiman.

According to the application of Raja Bal Krishna Reddi, it is stated that he is not in a position to pay the amount fixed by the Government due to the failure of monsoons and disturbance of the loan payments. Hence, *pargana* Amarchinta and *pargana* Waddiman (with all taxes) along with the revenue, excess revenue, excise, professional taxes, *sibandi*, stationery, goats for Idd-uz-zuha, *rusum* registrar, head *deshpandyagiri* and *rusum* have been entrusted to him for an amount of Rs 5,000 for 1836–37. Therefore, he must now be satisfied and gain the confidence of the old and new ryots. He must rehabilitate the above-mentioned *pargana* and make it financially sound. This is a reliable order.

ꕤ

No. 16
1838–39

Copy of the rulings under the seal of Raja Chandu Lal Maharaja Bahadur.

Raja Gopal Rao Bahadur, *deshmukh* of *sarkar* Pangal.

Raja Sahib

It is evident that for the administration of *rusum watan*, Raja Ram Parshad Lala Bahadur was appointed registrar of *taluq* Gopalpet in 1834–35. Till then, no arrangements for the *rusum* and other sources of revenue of the *pargana* have been made. Therefore, this is to state that as soon as this order is received, the *rusum*, 10 per cent *jama kamil* and two *begas* of land per village with *man-o-pan* and the record keeper's signature, etc., that pertain to you in the villages of the *jagirdars* of the above-said *pargana* may be fixed from 1835–36 and sent to the agent of the aforesaid Raja. A receipt for the same may be obtained.

No. 17
1839–40

Gracious Raja Sahib Raja Rameshwar Rao Bahiri Bahadur Esq.
From Syed Ameen Diwan, Salaam.

All is well here, and please be writing about your well-being. Now we have sent a peon Doulath Khan for our salary pertaining to the year 1839–40. Our salary may be accounted in consultation with Venkaiah.

The salary for the year 1839–40	494
My own salary	400
Ameenulla Khan out of Rs 400	150
Interest on Rs 500/Rs of Sesha Rao	
Venkat Rao	40
Total	1,084

A sum of Rs 1,084 only may be sent immediately as soon as you receive this letter. The salaries of other people have been paid from our salaries, but our salaries have not been sent thus far. Now I am sending a peon. The amount may be sent through him. You are also similar to Raja Chandu Lal. You must have mercy upon us. A letter in reply may be sent along with the payments. Be it known to you.

No. 18
17 March 1840

Gracious Raja Sahib

An amount of Rs 2,950 towards the arrears of the salary of Mir Fasahat Ali, a horseman employed by the Government Risala since 23 August 1838 till the end of 23 August 1839, out of the revenue of *pargana* Sugur and Kothakota for the year 1838–39 is due to him. Hence, the amount may be paid to him in instalments during this year and a disbursement register prepared as per rules may be maintained. At present, according to the Government order, the entries may be taken in the account book.

ꝏ

No. 19
12 April 1840

Seal
Mir Maujud Ali

An amount of Rs 1,900 (the half of which amounts to Rs 950) towards the arrears of my salary as calculated from the revenue of *tehsil pargana* Sugur and Kothakota for the year 1839–40 has been received from Sawai Raja Rameshwar Rao Bahiri Bahadur, *deshmukh* of the above-mentioned *pargana*, in consultation with his agent. The same has been spent towards my personal expenses. Hence, this is executed as a receipt of disbursement to be used whenever required.

ꙮ

No. 20
26 November 1840

Gracious Raja Sahib

After the eagerness to see you, this is to state that your letter sent through Ghalib Khan Afghan, along with 400 guavas and twelve pomegranates is received, and the state of affairs are known by reading the letter. I shall be happy if you keep me informed about your well-being. For the appointment of *jawan*s, Muslims may be called for and sent here. They shall be appointed on a salary of Rs 8 per month. However, the *jawan*s should be tall, handsome, and between eighteen and nineteen years.

ꙮ

No. 21
1840–41

Gracious Raja Sahib

A Majlis has been set up at the capital Hyderabad, Farkhunda Bunyad, for the settlement of cases concerning the troops of the *ilaqadar*s, *ziladar*s and *taluqdar*s, and for the punishment of wrongdoers.

Therefore, this is written to state that on receipt of these orders and the enclosed letter from the aforesaid Majlis, every case concerning the troops, maintained to deal with the punishment of troublemaking Rohillas, plundering *ziladar*s, robbery in your *ilaqa* or any other kind of trouble, must be reported. Some measures that you have used in the past for the prevention of crime, and which you think are proper, may also be suggested to the Majlis in your letter. In reply to your letter, the Majlis will give some advice regarding those cases and you must act accordingly. The accounts of *wasul baqi*, personal salaries and the expenses of the troops may, however, be kept with you.

Letters and covers addressed to the above-mentioned Majlis should not bear titles of honour (forms of address). You may only use this form of address: 'For the information of the members of the Majlis, who decide cases involving troops employed by the *ilaqadar*s, *ziladar*s and *taluqdar*s, for subduing mischievous elements.' You must number your letters, starting from one and increasing a number for each letter, till the end of the year. Your year must start from the first day of Muharram.

1841

No. 22
8 January 1841

Gracious Raja Sahib

An amount of Rs 6,800 towards the arrears of the salary of Mir Qamaruddin Khan, a horseman employed by the Government Risala since the month of 22 August 1840 till the end of 21 August 1841, out of the revenue of *pargana* Sugur and Kothakota for the year 1840–41 is due to him. Hence, in instalments the amount may be paid to him during this year and a disbursement register prepared as per rules may be maintained. At present, according to the Government order, the entries may be taken in the account book.

No. 23
1841

Gracious Raja Sahib

After best compliments and eagerness to see you, this is to state that while I was waiting for your letter, I received a letter written in Telugu that informed me about the state of affairs. Mirza Muhammad Ali Baig has been appointed there by a *sanad* and by official orders. It is necessary that you contact him and act according to the Government orders. The revenue of *tehsildari*, etc., for the year 1841–42 is Rs 8,000 and the arrears of 1840–41 are Rs 2,000. Hence, a total amount of Rs 10,000 may be arranged. Since 31 July 1840, Government orders will also be issued regarding the revenue. According to the Government, at the end of Zilhaj of the same year, seven months would have passed and for that period you would have to pay only Rs 1,610 as revenue, and from 23 February 1841 you may have to pay Rs 230 monthly. You may feel happy to know that every effort will be made to act according to your wishes and to increase the feelings of affection and friendship between us. Our friendship would cease if I do not receive the amount and if you pay revenue to the Government instead, in which case I would be compelled to live on the friendship without my salary. This is not good. Rs 8 towards the expenses of the *taluq* may be sent monthly starting from 25 December 1840, so that cases of the people may be dealt with. Mirza Sahib and Abdullah have stated something that may be complied with. They said that an amount of Rs 500 may be paid by Ali Bin Sayeed to the *tehsildar* every month and a receipt may be obtained from him. The rest is well.

No. 24
1841–42

Gracious Sri Sawai Raja Rameshwar Rao Bahiri Balwant Deshmukh *pargana* Sugur, etc.

From your friend, Shyama Raidu, blessings.

All is well here. Please be writing about the pleasures at your side. The salary of Basharath Khan, horseman, for the year 1841–42 amounting to

Rs 250 is included in the estimate. Now that amount is given to the post created in the area of Mir Ashik Hussain. Therefore, it is informed. You have to pay an amount of Rs 500 in total to Mir Sahib. See that the case in this regard may not come to this level. That is all.

No. 25
1841–42

Gracious Sri Sawai Raja Rameshwar Rao Bahiri Balwant Deshmukh *pargana* Sugur, etc.

From Mir Mouzood Ali Sahib, Salaam.

All is well here. Please be writing about the pleasures at your side. Further, you have sent the list of receipts and arrears of revenue for the period of two years along with this letter; so the letter written on 9 October was received on 12 October through your *jawan*s and the contents noted. The bi-annual list of receipts and arrears of revenue that was prepared and sent to us is not convincing. The previous list of the revenue receipts, to the extent of cash payments, certified page by page, is present with us. If the list for the year 1840–41 is separately written in accordance with the previously certified list of revenue receipts, it may be sent to us so that it can be verified with the list that is kept with us. The collection list of cash payment for the year 1841–42 was submitted to us through Mirza Muhammad Ali Baig. At present, the commendation from Nazeer Muhammad Khan is received. The copies of the previous list of revenue receipts written by you must be present in your office. In accordance with them, the list of total receipts and arrears for the years 1832–33 and 1833–34 may be prepared separately for each year in the presence of the aforesaid Khan and dispatched to us. Further, you have written that the *jawans* of Raja Ujagar Chand Rai Bahadur have come. Our amount of Rs 2,000 for the year 1832–33 is due from you. From that amount, Rs 1,000 may be adjusted to the *jawan*s of Rai Bahadur. The payment for the year 1833–34 should not be paid, not even a single *paisa*. The *jawan*s should also be informed that there is a ban from the Government and the cash has also been remitted to the Government; in spite of all this, if you make the payment to them, you have to pay them again. The Telugu letters of Karivenu Laxmaiah Venkatapathi are sent to you. The Honourable Minister is not present in the city. He has come to you. Therefore, the letters in return have been handed over to your *jawans*. Be it known to you. If there are any objections in the process of collections, one of the *jawans* from these may be sent here, so that it may be settled face to face. The amount of our Khan pertaining to the descriptive roll has not been sent by you so far. This seems to be most surprising. Even after sending the orders several times from here, your silence on this issue and not sending the amount seems to be really surprising. So the amount of arrears may be paid immediately. A period of three months in the second year has also elapsed, and debts have been increasing. Despite writing several letters for the salary of former Mirza Fatheulla Baig, the payment was not sent by you. On enquiry, you have said to that gentleman, it seems, that you have given the said payment to Mouzood Ali. When did you give the payment to me? Such sort of improper statements of yours to the salaried people, I think, shall create some misunderstanding between the employees and us. These things may be avoided. Anyhow, the salary of the aforesaid Mirza may be paid.

No. 26
20 February 1842

Gracious Raja Sahib

According to the payroll, out of the revenue of *pargana* Sugur and Kothakota for the year 1841–42, an amount of Rs 360, being the arrears of the salary of Sheikh Karimuddin Bargir, employed by the Government in the *ilaqa* of Dilpat Rai, is due to him. Hence, the amount must be paid to him in instalments during this year and a disbursement register prepared according to the rules must be maintained. At present, according to the Government order, the entries may be taken in the account book.

1843 

No. 27
25 January 1843

An amount of Rs 1,850 towards the arrears of the salary of Ghulam Dastagir Sufidposh, horseman, employed by the Government Risala from 21 August 1842 till the end of 20 August 1843, out of the revenue of *pargana* Sugur and Kothakota for the year 1842–43 is due to him. Hence, the amount may be paid to him in instalments during this year and a disbursement register prepared as per rules may be maintained. At present, according to the Government order, the entries may be taken in the account book.

ꕤ

No. 28
2 June 1843

Gracious Sri Sawai Raja Rameshwar Rao Bahiri Balwant Deshmukh *pargana* Sugur, etc.

From your friend, Rai Lakshma Raidu, blessings.

All is well here, and please be writing about the pleasures at your side. The salary of Deedar Baig, a sum of Rs 925 pertaining to the years 1841–43, is included in the estimate. The said person has submitted an appeal to the Government. Therefore, the orders from the Government have been issued. The amount was paid by Ganga Singh Kundan. Hence, it was written by him. As soon as you receive this letter, please send the amount in cash to the *jawan*s of Ganga Singh. Previously an amount of Rs 75 pertaining to the salary of Muhammad Thaqui Khan payable to Muhammad Ameer Khan Bakshi was not paid until today. It is said that these paid servants are going to complain in the court of the Gracious Raja Sahib. Therefore, the special attendants Venkaiah and Ramahiah are being sent with orders. As such, the salaries of Ganga Singh Kundan and Bekhshi Sahib may be paid and receipts be taken. There are frequent complaints from the paid servants. Therefore, proper arrangements may be made. Raja Rai Bahadur also wrote a letter. More is known through the letter. These special attendants Venkaiah and Ramaiah may be paid at the rate of Rs 1 per day.

1844

No. 29
1844–45

Gracious Raja Sahib

It is obvious that the annual amount for the year 1843–44 towards *mauza* Kondanagula in *pargana* Godal, which is *zat jagir* of Mirza Ali Muhammad, son of Muhammad Jung Bahadur, is due from you. Therefore, without making any excuses, you must now send the amount mentioned above to the Naib Bahadur and submit the receipt for the same to the Government. You must take this as a strict order, and this must be known to the Government.

ꟹ

No. 30
1844–45

Your Highness

In consultation with a Government order, with the opinion of Muhammad Namdar Khan, an order has been sent to the *deshmukh*s and *deshpande*s of the places surrounding your *ilaqa*. Therefore, you must refer to the aforesaid Khan and have the *panchayat* decide about the portion belonging to Chaudhar Reddi, *zamindar* of Godal. This is a Government memo.

ꟹ

No. 31
1844–45

Gracious Raja Sahib

You have sent Venkat Vakil to handle your administrative matter after having made all the arrangements. He is aware of all the details of the report. However, you should always write the informal letters personally.

No. 32
1845–46

Seal: rectangular
Raja Khushal Chand
Fidvi Asaf Jah

Gracious Raja Sahib

Your *vakil* came with all your letters, and the details of the report are known. I forwarded the letters to the Government without any delay. I shall give your application to the Raja Sahib when he arrives. The administration of the Government in the capital was found to be satisfactory by the Raja. The Government must not be blamed for any delay in the payment of the salaries of the employees. In future, you must not keep their salaries in arrears either. Kindly send your statement in this regard without delay.

There are other explanations that you need to give in your statement. It has come to my knowledge that you plundered the village and devastated it. You must restrain from such activities and try to be fair. I pray to God to show you the right path.

ഌ

No. 33
1845–46

Gracious Raja Sahib

It is evident that Mahur was given the amount due towards the compensation and the salaries of the clerks and the Government employees of the *iluqa* of Sham Rao, for the years 1842–43 and 1843–44. However, the salaries have not been paid to them yet, which is disgraceful. Therefore, as soon as you receive this order, the compensation and the salaries of the clerks must be paid and a receipt obtained from them. This is a strict Government memo.

ꙮ

No. 34
1845–46

Seal: rectangular
Maharaja Chandulal

Gracious Raja Sahib

Abdullah bin Ali Khan Mudassir Jung has to pay Rs 3,000 towards the salary of Mir Ahmed Ali Khan for the year 1841–42 out of the revenue of *pargana* Sugur and Kothakota. Therefore, I assume that you have paid the Khan and obtained a receipt from him. The necessary entries must be made in the account book.

ꙮ

No. 35
1845–46

Gracious Raja Sahib

After expressing my eagerness to see you, this is to state that *pargana* Sugur and other *mahal*s have been assigned to you by the Government. You have sent in this connection Seshachalam, Lakshmaiah and your agent Venkat Rao. Therefore, this is to state that according to the calculations done by the aforesaid Rao, you had to pay the amount due to the Government along with arrears to which you had agreed in your sealed letter. On enquiring, it was found that you have not paid the arrears. Only the amount mentioned in your agreement has been paid. Therefore, you must pay the arrears as well, and let this loyal friend report to the Government that you have paid the entire amount owed to the Government. May you prosper by day and remain loyal to the Government. For the rest, all is well. Your agent will make you aware of the other details.

1846

No. 36
1846

Gracious Raja Sahib

I was happy to receive your letter dated 26 January 1846. You have not yet repaid the moneylenders. Since you did not keep your promise, they have approached me. The decision regarding this will be taken after five or six days, and it will be binding on you. Hence, you must somehow repay the amount that you owe to the Government and to the moneylenders before that. Only then would the Government be pleased. The moneylenders seem to be perplexed by your verbal statements.

The case regarding the village of Rachala is pending owing to your carelessness. This is not proper. It must be decided soon. Balwant Rao and your *vakil*s may be sent here, so that they can be consulted about this case and a piece of advice for the maintenance of the *samasthan* may also be given to them. You must work for the welfare of the *samasthan*.

ജ

No. 37
18 August 1846

Under the special seal of Sawai Raja Rameshwar Rao Bahiri Balwant Bahadur who had taken a loan from Goji Ram and Sada Sukh Sahu, residents of Bagh with the consent of Elchi Rao and Gopalji Rao.

Received an amount of Rs 2,000 out of which Rs 1,666 and 8 *anna*s only are taken as interest on the previous amount and the remaining Rs 333 and 8 *anna*s are credited to the account of the above-mentioned.

ꟸ

No. 38
12 September 1846

To the Risaladar Sahib

A letter with orders from Raja Ram Baksh and one from the Resident have been received. It is learnt that troublemaking Narsimha Reddi has crossed the Krishna River along with four persons from the village of Kavil Kanka. It is suspected that he might have taken shelter in Wanaparthy or around that *taluq*. He must be arrested and sent to the capital. Therefore, this is to state that efforts to trace him and arrest him must be made. Please make a note of the description of the criminal and his age before beginning the search.

The Resident has sent three letters here with orders. It is learnt that 250 Rohillas have absconded from Akola cantonment. In case they have taken shelter in our *taluq*s, they are to be arrested and sent to Makhtal cantonment. Hence, this is to state that as soon as you receive this letter, you must try to arrest them with the help of your troops wherever they are and send them to the commandant of the above-said cantonment because this is the order of the Resident.

[Signed] Raja Sahib

No. 39
20 September 1846

Received a letter of recommendation from the Government in reply to your application stating that you may be permitted to go to the *taluq* of Wanaparthy. A copy of the letter along with a copy of the letter attached to it and the copy of the reply from this side written today to Siraj-ul-Mulk Bahadur is enclosed. If you are not well, you may go to your *taluq*. The road tax permit with our seal and signature from our side is enclosed. However, until the reply to the result of your suit is sent to the Government, you cannot leave for your *taluq*. It would not be proper on our part to grant you permission to go to your *taluq* until then. We would also not advise you to leave until then.

ꙮ

No. 40
20 September 1846

Received a letter of recommendation from Siraj-ul-Mulk Bahadur addressed to the Honourable Resident General Fraser Bahadur, dated 24th of the present month, along with an application submitted by Raja Rameshwar Rao, the *zamindar* of Wanaparthy, asking for permission to return back to Wanaparthy owing to his ill health.

Fateh Khan and others have filed suit against you and have appealed for justice. Hence, in accordance with the request in your application dated 4 September, the *zamindar* mentioned above will attend the *panchayat* to have his case settled. An agreement with your seal, according to the draft enclosed with it, stating your acceptance and willingness is filed in the office. Your application is returned herewith.

ꙮ

No. 41
20 September 1846

Copy of a letter of recommendation from the Honourable Resident General Fraser Bahadur.

To Siraj-ul-Mulk Bahadur

The letter of recommendation in reply to my friend's letter mentions that Fateh Khan had filed a suit against the *zamindar* and had appealed for justice. The final decision was given by the *panchayat*, and it was accepted by the *zamindar* according to the draft enclosed herewith, which carries his seal. These documents have been sent to the Government office. The *zamindar* now returned to Wanaparthy. You had sent for the *zamindar* mentioned above and helped him to settle his matters. I have also reached a settlement with him. However, you did not mention anything about the other cases at that time. Since the *zamindar* mentioned above was present, he could have all those suits settled that were filed by some other clerks of the Government. Hence, the above-mentioned *zamindar* went on leave to *taluq* Wanaparthy with his own road tax permit.

This is to state in friendly terms that the draft of the agreement enclosed herewith is being brought to your knowledge. Rohillas have also been mentioned about which you were not aware till now, which is a good sign. It also mentions that only fifty Telugu people were in the *jawan*s category. In your letter, you must also make mention of the suit filed against the *zamindar* of Gurmatkal. You must also mention this after some arrangement is made by the Government and the *taluqdar*s.

Fateh Khan had filed a case against the *zamindar* because the latter did not meet his demands since he had no orders from the Government. As a rule, the *zamindar* cannot act unless he has orders from the Government. This rule was made in order to safeguard the position of all the *zamindar*s, *taluqdar*s and *naib*s.

ℵ

No. 42
15 October 1846

Seal: rectangular

Order in the name of Sawai Raja Gopal Rao Bahadur, *deshmukh* and *deshpande* of *pargana* Haveli, *sarkar* Pangal.

According to the request of the aforesaid Bahadur, village Edolapally in *pargana* Haveli in the above-mentioned *sarkar subah* Farkhunda Bunyad, Hyderabad, for an amount of Rs 2,000 excluding the expenses towards *sibandi*, stationery, *rusum*, etc., along with *khilat* has been given on lease order for the year 1846–47. Now you can be at peace and try to win the favour of the old and the new ryots. You must improve the cultivation of the land. The amount due to the Government must be paid according to fixed instalments. You must obtain receipts for the same. No changes must be made in the above-mentioned amount. This is a reliable order.

ꙮ

No. 43
1846

Gracious Raja Sahib

After expressing eagerness to see you and having prayed for you, this is to let you know that I am well here and pray for your well-being. This is to report that after you had departed along with the cavalry and Sherao Deshmukh on 26 January 1846 and entered [illegible], Yallanna Deshmukh did not come here. Instead, he took your *jawan* with him to the capital. He wants to submit a detailed report. He has taken some documents from the aforesaid Bahadur and sent them. However, the claim made by Yellanna is yet to be considered. This is for your information. My best wishes to the Raja Sahib.

ꙮ

No. 44
1846–47

Vanma Sakiram, village Suddapalle, fixed rate village of Devarakonda, Venkata Ramaiah year 1846–47, principal amount Kartheeka Budi 13.

323 fixed rate amount for the whole year.

Misc:
6 Duty of Ranga Swami
1 for writing Diwanji
6-8-0 To Sheristadar Rao
6-4-6 Dassera presentations
Total: 19-12-6

Total: 343-12-6

5-4-0 Zakir for misc. expend.

Grand Total: 348-0-6

Expenditure:

323 As per Government account
6 To Sri Ranga Swami as per the account of Srirangapur
1 To Sri Diwanji for writing
6-8-0 To Sheristadar Rao
6-4-6 Dassera presentations to Vennacheru
5-4-0 The expenditure incurred in connection with the ryots and accountants of rural areas
348-0-6 Total

ഇ

No. 45
1846–47

Seal: rectangular
Raja Chandulal

Young one, be blessed.

Venkat Vakil of Sawai Raja Rameshwar Rao Bahadur came to the office of the Government and had that case settled. Now, you may leave the place with your troops and proceed toward the boundaries of Palmoor, but you must not harm or trouble anyone there.

ഇ

No. 46
1846

This is a description of Ari Mari Raman Chanchu who fled after wounding five people on 19 May 1846. Of those wounded, one girl, the daughter of Fakhru Khan, has died. The murderer is a resident of Bulore Wausham Puldiya Maresham *taluq* Nandkana. Ari belongs to the Gond caste. He is of average height, and bears marks on his waist and both his thumbs. He also stammers.

ꙮ

No. 47
1846–47

Raja Chandu Lal Bahadur

Young one, be blessed.

Prior to this, two letters were issued ordering you to break camp and leave Narsari village. You were instructed to stay at Gopalpet and not to collect hay and provisions, etc., from the village in the *taluq* of Sugur and Kothakota, which is the *ilaqa* of Raja Rameshwar Rao Bahadur. This is to state that in spite of these orders, you did not break camp nor did you stop collecting hay and provisions, etc., from the village in Sugur and Kothakota. Hence, two Government servants are being sent to compel you to move from Narsari village and restrain you from collecting hay and provisions from the *ilaqa* of the aforesaid Raja in the future. Therefore, as soon as the Government servants arrive, you must break camp and leave for Gopalpet, and stop collecting hay and provisions. The consequences will be harmful in case you make any excuses. This is a strict Government order.

No. 48
1846–47

Gracious Raja Sahib

A letter from Muhammad Baig, *jamedar*, enclosed with a handwritten receipt addressed to Syed Ali Musa Raza, *taluqdar*, has been received. It is hoped that this letter will not be taken as the last letter and that communication will continue between them. It is learnt that some of the horsemen have been dismissed. I fear my horsemen are also in trouble. I forwarded the letter and the receipt to the *taluqdar*, but as the contents of the letter were inflammatory, the *jamedar* did not attend to the matter. Hence, the contents were changed, and when this letter was sent, the matter was taken up. The horsemen submitted a memorandum in which it was mentioned that since the Minister of Revenue was not pleased with the present horsemen, he dismissed them and appointed others in their place. Moreover, he has sent for the list of newly appointed horsemen to be submitted to the Raja Sahib for his approval and for the compensation of the horsemen to be fixed. The aforesaid *jamedar* expects his personal case to be decided soon at a time when the Government is concerned about the administration of the entire Risala. The orders that have been passed in consultation with this side must not be changed, and one must not be impatient with the Government.

No. 49
3 August 1847

Gracious Raja Sahib

It has been informed by the Government that your witnesses, Sheikh Ghalib and Sardar Khan, are present here. This is to inform you that they are being sent by the Government at half past one. Therefore, you may be present tomorrow at the above-mentioned time.

ꕥ

No. 50
13 August 1847

Gracious Raja Sahib

The Government order enclosed with this letter has been received and has made me aware of the facts.

༄

No. 51
16 September 1847

Seal: rectangular
Naqi Khan Bahadur

Order executed in the name of the businessmen and other well-wishers of Rachala village in the *ilaqa* of Subba Reddi, *deshmukh* and *nar'gaur* of *pargana* Kandur, *sarkar* Ghanapur. In confirmation of your application, the order has been granted to you. Therefore, you must now be satisfied and establish yourself in the village mentioned above. You must engage yourself in business and pay the village artisan tax annually. This order is reliable.

༄

No. 52
February/March 1847

An amount of Rs 15,000 (the half of which amounts to Rs 7,500) towards the cultivation of crops in Rachala, as detailed below, has been received through Ghulam Naqi according to the instalments fixed. This amount has to be sent to Deshmukhni Mundari and the document must be taken back. These few words have been written to be preserved as a document. Any other document besides this would not be valid.

1848

No. 53
10 February 1848

Draft of the Faisalnama regarding the ruin of village Rachala, *pargana* Kandur.

According to the Government orders, Bandi Lakshma Rao, Balwant Rao Inspector, Cochakla Krishna Reddi, *deshmukh* and *nar'gaur* of *pargana* Nagarkurnool, and Tum Paras Ram Reddi, *deshmukh* and *nar'gaur* of Haveli Ghanapur, came to the above-said village along with Sawai Raja Rameshwar Rao Balwant Bahiri Bahadur Deshmukh, *deshpande* and *nar'gaur* of *pargana* Sugur, etc., Malyal Seshachalam Sardar and Karuna Lakshmiah, agent. The aforesaid Raja Sahib and Soma Reddi, the adopted son of Rai Bolai, *deshmukh* of *pargana* Kandur, along with Kotaiah Mutiyanam and the agent Sanganna came and called the people. In the presence of the Asamies, the case pertaining to the ruin of the village Rachala was examined. After that, in the presence of the plaintiffs, defendants and other Asamies of Rachala, it was decided that the *deshmukh* be transferred to Rai Bolai Deshmukh from the aforesaid Raja.

[Signatures]

ஐ

No. 54
18 February 1848

[Copy of the document under the seal of Siraj-ul-Mulk Bahadur]

To the *deshmukhs*, *deshpandes*, registrars, headmen, *kulkarnis*, ryots and cultivators.

The following villages that had been purchased by Raja Krishna Rao in 1847–48 according to the old tradition have been continued in the name of Raja Rameshwar Rao Bahadur. Therefore, the *deshmukh* of the above-named place may consider the Raja to be permanent and pay the *rusum*, necessaries, dependencies, other sources of revenue, *inam*, fixed rate lands and *man-o-pan* as usual. The means of the aforesaid *deshmukh* is through the right of necessaries, which he may spend on improving the cultivation of the village, providing of the village, and winning the favour of the old and new ryots. He must approach the officials and the *jagirdar*s and pay the fixed and proper revenue in time. This is a strict Government memo.

ꙮ

No. 55
23 July 1848

Gracious Raja Sahib

Your application requesting that you should be excused for not being able to attend the court owing to your ill health was given full consideration. However, your absence from the court affected the work of the Government to a great extent and caused inconvenience to the other people who had come to give evidence. Nevertheless, the court was adjourned for today but you must be present on Monday at about three o'clock.

ꙮ

No. 56
4 September 1848

Stamp of the Revenue Office

[Copy of the *sanad* under the seal of Siraj-ul-Mulk Bahadur]

To the revenue collectors, *jagirdar*s, *deshmukh*s, *deshpandes*, headmen and accountants of *pargana* Narkhoda, *pargana* of Haveli Muhammadnagar Sarkar above-mentioned and *pargana* of Burgul Sarkar Kilkonda, *subah* Farkhunda Bunyad, Hyderabad.

The above-mentioned people are hereby informed by the Royal Court that since the cultivated lands of Ramkishtapur, etc., had been purchased by the ancestors of Raja Rameshwar Rao Bahiri Balwant Bahadur, *deshmukh, deshpande, nar'gaur* and head *maniwar* of *pargana* Sugur and Kothakota, etc., the aforesaid Raja of the above-mentioned *subah* was entrusted with an amount of Rs 357 with goods, excise, village artisan tax, etc., under the head fixed rate revenue. Therefore, the aforesaid Raja must take possession of the hamlets mentioned below and pay the revenue tax on these annually and cropwise as usual according to tradition. This is an order that should be complied with.

ᘓ

No. 57
1848

Seal: rectangular
Siraj-ul-Mulk

Gracious Raja Sahib

From the application of Muhammad Ameenuddin, *naib* of *pargana* Jatprole, dated 12 March 1848, it is evident that your *ilaqadar*s are trying to find the lost ponies (large in size) of village Baswaipalle in *pargana* Koilkonda within the limits of village Sugur in *pargana* Nagarkurnool. The ponies were stolen while they were being driven to the bazaar of Janumpet to be sold, so that *zamindarni* of Janimalli, Nagarkurnool, Baqqal, could repay the loan given to her. Hence, the bullocks of the ryots of village Karpally in the *pargana* mentioned above have been brought here by force. This is not right. You must try to trace the ponies that have been taken away by the aforesaid grain merchant. In case the ponies are traced to village Sugur, the *maniwar* of that village has to give an explanation for this; otherwise the Government would arrest him. Since the aforesaid *zamindarni* has to repay the loan to the grain merchant, he must recover the amount from her. In case of any disagreement or quarrel, the case must be taken to the court and decided there, like it is done in the case of robbers and transgressors. It is not proper to take away the bullocks that are useful to the ryots for drawing water from the wells. Therefore, on receipt of this order, the bullocks mentioned above may be returned to the aforesaid ryots in consultation with the *naib* of Nagarkurnool and a receipt for the same may be obtained. This should not be difficult for you.

1849

No. 58
23 November 1849

Seal: illegible

This is written to present and future revenue collectors of *pargana* Devarkadra. After the death of Subba Reddi, son of Sawai Rai Mallai, the *watan deshmukhi* and *nar'gauri* of *patti* of Rachala in the above-mentioned *pargana* have been restored by the kindness of the Royal Court to Venkat Siva Reddi, the adopted son of Venkai, wife of the aforesaid late Subba Reddi, from the beginning of the year 1849–50. After Venkat Siva Reddi, the *watan deshmukhi* and *nar'gauri* will be restored to his sons and heirs. According to the tradition, this will continue from generation to generation. Therefore, Venkat Siva Reddi may consider himself the permanent *deshmukh* and *nar'gaur* and may continue to receive and spend the salary *rusum*, other sources of revenue, etc., and the necessaries of hereditary rights mentioned above, according to the tradition. He may use the income from the salary *rusum*, other sources of revenue, etc., and *huquq* hereditary rights *malikana* for his personal expenses. He must win the favour of the old and the new ryots by treating them well. He must make an effort to improve the cultivation and rehabilitate the village. In carrying out his duties, he must be obedient and loyal and active and must pay the revenue taxes regularly after every crop. This is an order and must be strictly complied with.

1850

No. 59
1850

Gracious Raja Sahib

From the Resident Bahadur's letter and the memo from the Commissariat of Mysore, it is learnt that 350 horses are being brought here from

Mysore by way of Kothakota. They left Mysore on 2 or 3 February 1850. Therefore, you may kindly arrange for 135 *maunds* or 31 *seers* horse gram or *kulthi*, 350 bundles of grass, 100 iron pegs and grain for 400 men. Whatever else they require may also be provided to them, at the price agreed upon. Precautions must be taken to see that no complaint of any kind in this regard comes to the Government.

ᢀ

No. 60
21 July 1850

Seal
To Raja Ram Krishna Rao Bahadur

Gracious Raja Sahib

The old documents like the *sanad* Niyabat-i-diwani and the *sanad* issued by Raja Chandu Lal Bahadur have been examined. From this, it is evident that you are minting the coins in Sugur and have brought them for circulation in the Government treasury and in your entire territory. Hence, as per the old tradition, formal permission is being given to you by the Government to mint the coins in Sugur. Therefore, you may now mint the coins just as is being done in Gadwal and Narayanpet.

ᢀ

No. 61
29 September 1850

Draft of the letter from Nawab Shah Yar-ul-Mulk.

Today I camped in the garden of Raja Sir Rao outside Golipur. You are aware of the fact that I live in difficult circumstances. I have no other place to go to other than yours. You are my master in every respect. Although I am away from you, I am entirely dependent on you for support.

ᢀ

No. 62
4 October 1850

Seal
Ghulam Muhammad Khan

Order in the name of Sawai Raja Venkat Gopal Rao Bahiri Bahadur, *deshmukh* and *deshpande* of Nar'khora *pargana*, Haveli *sarkar* Pangal, *subah* Farkhunda Bunyad, Hyderabad.

According to your application, Samvandla village in the above-said *pargana*, Haveli Madnur, is hereby given on order for an amount of Rs 2,300 from the beginning of 1850–51. Therefore, you must make a sincere effort to keep the ryots happy and to improve the cultivation. You must pay the instalments according to the agreement and obtain receipts for the same. This is a valid order.

No. 63
12 January 1851

Gracious Raja Sahib

The *naib* has received two letters from the Arabs. In one, they have threatened to plunder the *jatra*, and in the other, to obtain an order. We have already written to the *naib* about his departure for the *jatra*. Why are you afraid? Do you have any news of the city? A message of encouragement may be sent to them. You may also send your *vakil* to the city to gather information. Let him stay in one place and send his servant to get news of the city. He can send it over to you through him. In spite of this warning, if the *jatra* is still plundered, it will be happy news, because you will reap what you have sown.

ꕥ

No. 64
7 February 1851

Ghulam Mohiuddin Khan, son of Ashraf Khan, occupation Arab Khan, was appointed by you last year.

On 22 December, all of a sudden at midnight, thieves attacked the Khan's house in the neighbouring village. They entered the house and escaped with all his belongings. This is to inform you that I am a witness to it.

ꙮ

No. 65
12 February 1851

Gracious Raja Sahib

Your letter dated 6 February 1851 addressed to Govind Naik Sahu and the order enclosed, sent through your horsemen and the Arabs, has been received. Another letter sent earlier through six horsemen and the Arabs that was addressed to your *naib* has also been received.

ꙮ

No. 66
14 March 1851

Gracious Raja Sahib

After expressing my eagerness to see you, this is to state that your letter dated 10 March 1851 has been received by the *naib*. It is evident that you are going to attend the *jatra* of Srirangapur in person and hence want the *naib* to return. Therefore, on 13 March 1851, a letter was sent to inform you that the *naib* is returning. Another letter that is enclosed with it is addressed to the *naib*, asking him to send the *vakil* as per the instructions given. As for attending the *jatra*, there is no harm in partaking of it for your good self. I send my best wishes and pray for your happiness.

ꙮ

No. 67
25 March 1851

Gracious Raja Sahib

The letter dated 21 March 1851 states that the Arabs are treating debtors cruelly. The detailed report of facts that they are looting and plundering the place has come to my attention. A small contingent has been sent from the rear side, and whatever else is required would be sent, but you must bear the expenses of all the arrangements that will be made, otherwise the *taluq* would go into difficulty. In case you are unable to arrange for the amount, you must write to the office soon so that this matter could be brought to the notice of the Government and I personally could come there. However, you must not feel embarrassed, but send the reply very soon.

Furthermore, this is written in a friendly spirit and has nothing to do with the Arabs. This is only by way of friendship.

ꙮ

No. 68
6 August 1851

Copy.
Respected Sri Karivenu Laxmaiah Esq.
Salutations.

In consultation with Sri Bansi Raj Girdhari Prasad, we are going to prepare a document for the allotment of fallow land at Donur village as a resource for the purpose of 'Nitya Kainkaryam', i.e., for the day-to-day divine services in the temple. Therefore, after being shown the said land by you, they will build a village and bring the said land under plough, while collecting the new and old ryots around for settlement. Further, they will also construct tanks and wells for their development. We shall prepare the document and give it to them after fixing the revenue, i.e., for the fixed rate as well as the boundaries for the said land as fixed by you. Now by giving this fixed rate, you would be helping perform the every day divine services of Swami for generation after generation. Be it known to you.

1852

No. 69
23 November 1852

Seal
In the name of [illegible]

Devarakonda Venkaiah Mustazir, village Suddapalle, it is informed that the current year's second instalment of revenue, i.e., for the years 1852–53 of the said village has been sent in part payment, i.e., Rs 25, in the shape of a *hundi* and 12 *anna*s change separately. Therefore, this receipt will be issued after having the bank draft honoured with expenses.

ꙮ

No. 70
1852–53

To Azam Khan, *taluqdar* of *pargana* Sugur.

I was very happy to receive your letter through Narasimha, agent. If the contents of my previous letter were not satisfactory, then it is of no use to write about the problems regarding the case of the friend again and again. Enclosed with this letter is a petition to the Nawab Sahib, which will make you aware of all the details about the friend. At the request of the friend, the details about his case have also been sent to the highest authority. The friend shall feel very grateful if he receives a letter in reply to his petition.

ꙮ

No. 71
1852–53

Draft in reply to Lakshmi Das.

I received your letter and *chehra* through Venkoba Vakil and I learnt about the state of affairs. May God help Ausari Bhagwan and always keep him healthy and prosperous. Your *vakil* has made me fully aware of all your efforts. You must not hesitate to come to the Government office for help. You need not do anything under pressure from the Arab and Afghan *jawan*s to whom you have to pay the amount. You were exempted from the payment of dues to the Arabs once before. Your application has been submitted to the Nawab Sahib, along with a draft of the order. Keeping our friendship in view, the drafts of the papers that were submitted to the Government and a letter of the order are enclosed herewith.

ꟷ

No. 72
1852–53

Gracious Raja Sahib

According to the agent, the decision regarding the *patti* of Rachala was taken here for the year 1849–50. A communication regarding the same has been sent to you and will be reaching you soon. One village has been granted to you for your livelihood by the benevolence of the ruler. Therefore, you must pay the amount fixed in instalments to Muhammad Ruknuddin Khan Bahadur. These orders must be complied with.

No. 73
17 November 1853

According to the tradition, the annual amount of Rs 700 has been received in two equal instalments for the year 1851–52. The above-mentioned amount has been sent from the fixed rate lands in the *mauza* of Janwaram in the *pargana* of Sugur, fixed rate *ilaqa* of Sawai Raja Rameshwar Rao Balwant Bahiri Bahadur, *zamindar* of the above-mentioned *pargana*, on account of the confiscation of the *jagir* of Muhammad Ameen Khan. The amount has been paid to Janbaz Jung Bahadur.

ꟸ

No. 74
9 February 1853

Gracious Raja Sahib

It is learnt that the *maniwar* of Ambarpet and Chitralpally in the *pargana* of Nar'khora has been assigned to you from the beginning of the year 1852–53. You will be of help in all matters concerning the above-said villages.

[Signed] Raja Inderjit

No. 75
31 January 1854

I received your friendly letter, and by all means, I shall come personally before you and tell you all the details of the affairs. In all the matters of the Government in future, you may look into because I have no other person to help me except you. I hope that you would help me in all my affairs.

No. 76
2 March 1854

Draft of the application given to Nawab Salar Jung Bahadur.

I am your old and loyal servant. My ancestors have also been serving you for seven generations. It is my desire to pay my respects to you and spend my life serving you. However, due to persistent demands made by the Arabs and Afghan moneylenders, I was helpless. Before this, I was apprehended by the Arabs and suffered a great deal at their hands. Besides, I had to attend to lawsuits filed against me. For these reasons, I could not come personally and give you a detailed account of the matter.

I request you and beseech you to confirm the enclosed order by your favour and kindness. I will consider it an honour. I shall then come in your service with peace of mind and explain everything in detail to you. Your gracious grants will be the source of my livelihood because this devotee has no patron other than you. I shall always obey your orders. [In verse] 'If I have committed any crime, I put my head before you to forgive it.'

ꕤ

No. 77
7 May 1854

Order in the name of Suri Rai Mallaiah Deshmukhni of the *patti* Rachala, *pargana* of Kandur, *sarkar* Ghanapur, *subah* Farkhunda Bunyad, Hyderabad.

In accordance with the application of the aforesaid, and keeping in view the adjustment of the cost of rehabilitating the above-said *patti* in the *pargana*, *sarkar* and *subah* mentioned above, the goods, remaining revenue, liquor tax, village artisan tax, irrigated land, head public office, mango orchard, reaping, right of a deputy, village collector's fee, cultivator's produce, etc., under all heads numbering temporary except the *nazrana* portion and *rusum* in *sarbasta* have been assigned to her by the Government from the beginning of the year 1853–54 till the end of 1857–58, for a period of five years, for an amount of Rs 93,750 to be paid in equal annual instalments according to the details given below. Therefore, she must now be satisfied and try to gain the confidence of the old and the new ryots. She must rehabilitate the above-mentioned *patti* in the *pargana*, *sarkar* and *subah* mentioned above, pay the fixed instalments annually to the Government and obtain receipts for the same. This is an authentic order.

ℬ𝒪

No. 78
10 May 1854

Order in the name of Maula Maddi Venkat Rama Reddi and Ram Krishna Reddi, *deshmukhs* of the *patti* of Chakkalmaddi, *pargana* of Kandur, *sarkar* Ghanapur, *subah* Farkhunda Bunyad, Hyderabad.

In accordance with the petition of the aforesaid people to provide subsistence to them with a livelihood and rehabilitate the *patti* in the above-mentioned *pargana*, *sarkar* and *subah* mentioned above, the goods, remaining revenue, village artisan tax, liquor tax, irrigated land, head public office, orchards and accounts, the right of *khilat*, road taxes, Government shares of produce, under all heads except *nazrana* portion and *rusum*, in order of *sarbasta* for a period of five years starting from the beginning of the year 1853–54 till the end of 1857–58 are sanctioned for an amount of Rs 93,750 according to the details mentioned below. This order under the seal of the Government is to confirm this. Therefore, you must now be satisfied and gain the confidence of the old and new ryots. According to the order, the excess revenue, etc., and the *patti* mentioned above in the above-said *pargana* must be rehabilitated, the above-mentioned amount should regularly be paid to the Government in annual instalments and receipts should be obtained for the same. In this regard, this order may be treated as trustworthy.

ℬ𝒪

No. 79
25 May 1854

Gracious Raja Sahib

It has come to our knowledge that a robbery was committed in Vespal village in the *jagir* of Mir Fida Hussain on 7 May 1854. Cash and belongings worth about Rs 400 were looted from a house in that hamlet. As the rights of district revenue have been entrusted to you, it is necessary for you to trace the thieves and arrest them, and recover the stolen articles. They must then be presented before the Government. Otherwise, you will have to compensate the loss. This is an order and must be complied with.

ꕤ

No. 80
27 June 1854

This is to state that with the consent of Kiyami Naik an amount of Rs 400 has been taken on loan from Yadgiri, village headman. Subsequently, my salary was fixed at Rs 5 from 27 June 1854.

The village of Ammapur, *sarkar* of Pangal, *pargana* of Vinukonda *jagir* was given for five years to him from 1852–53 for an amount of Rs 600 annually after deducting the *rusum* of Rs 85. I do hereby promise that the above-said village will be under my control till the amount is received. The amount is fixed and would be paid to me every month. In case the above-said village is taken away from me and given to others, I would pay off the remaining sum with interest at once after the accounts are compared and will not make any excuse. Hence, these few words have been executed to be used as an agreement when needed.

ꕤ

No. 81
10 July 1854

Gracious Raja Sahib

After expressing my eagerness to see you, this is to state that your application in reply to the Government letter has been received, through which I learnt about the state of affairs.

I also learnt that you are not keeping well. In a letter written in Telugu dated 14th of last month, you have mentioned that the doctor will be sent later. You have already sent the medicine prepared by the Munshi Sahib. Hence, kind sir, the doctor is not required for the time being, as the Munshi Sahib has advised me to fast. When I break the fast, I shall send for the doctor. At present I need two *tola*s of grape salt. I shall be grateful if you can kindly send it.

Azam Khan

ಐ

No. 82
23 July 1854

Seal

Niyabat-e-Diwanai
Nizam-ul-Mulk, Asaf Jah Bahadur

Order in the name of Papi Reddi, *deshmukh* of the *patti* of Kandur, *pargana* of Devarakonda, *sarkar* Ghanapur, *subah* Farkhunda Bunyad, Hyderabad.

In accordance with your petition and keeping in view your livelihood and the rehabilitation of the above-said *patti*, in the *pargana* and *sarkar* mentioned above, regarding the head descendants, liquor tax, tree tax, irrigated land, etc., along with *sibandi*, head expenses of the temple, *rusum*, the village stationery, etc., and all expenses of the palace in the way of *sarbasta*, it has been granted to you for a period of five years for an amount of Rs 31,250 to be paid in an equal instalment annually.

Now you must be satisfied and, taking the help of the old and new ryots, make an effort to improve the cultivation. The instalments to be paid to the Government in consultation with Venkat Gopal Reddi Deshmukh must be sent regularly every year and a receipt obtained for the same. The amount of the order should neither be increased nor decreased. This order may be deemed reliable. It must be complied with and action taken accordingly.

ಐ

No. 83
9 August 1854

Draft of the petition to Nawab Salar Jung Bahadur.

May you live long. I am your loyal servant and have served your ancestors as well. Due to untoward causes, I lost the means of my livelihood and have been a destitute for ten years. I thank God who fulfils the needs of the people. By his grace, I am still alive.

It was God's will that I should petition to you. All of a sudden, my fortune smiled on me. You are a just man and you contrived to solve my problems very easily. I had given up hope, but I have been made secure by your benevolence and by the grace of God. My entire life changed when my petition was sent to you for consideration. I am very grateful to you for having issued an order to Azam Khan, *taluqdar*, and his agent connected with my case to restore me to me the files, papers and the *sanad*s of my hereditary right of the *samasthan* according to the enclosed list. I consider it an honour. I promise to rehabilitate the *samasthan*. I shall always pray to God for your long life and prosperity.

Further, two of my servants have been imprisoned for their cowardliness. I shall be grateful if you write to Azam Khan to release them and also ask him to hand over the files, papers, other goods and arms to me. Besides these, there are four broken cannons and ten cannon balls that are not included in the list. All the *sanad*s and papers except the articles in the list are mortgaged in Kurnool. I shall be indebted to you if you issue orders to have them transferred back to my name. After my servants are released and after my papers and goods are restored to me, I shall send the list to you for you to go through it. I have already sent a copy of the list of the goods to the *taluqdar*.

This application is submitted in consultation with the *taluqdar*.

ဆ

No. 84
4 October 1854

Draft of the letter written to Nawab Salar Jung Bahadur.

Sometimes I keep the letter on my eyes and sometimes on my head. I received a letter and a Government order for which I was eagerly waiting. I shall come with my younger brother to pay homage to you. I am very grateful to you and feel with all humility that I cannot thank you adequately. I pray to God for your prosperity. I thought of coming personally, but I have not been well for some days and am running a high temperature. Azam Khan and Kishan Rao, *taluqdar*s of *sarkar* Pangal posted to the *pargana* of Sugur, also know about my illness as they had come to Wanaparthy. At that time, I was slightly better, but when I went to see the aforesaid Rao, I was taken seriously ill owing to the difficult and tiring journey. Hence, I came to Kurnool for medical treatment by Dr. Rogers. If, by the grace of God and with the doctor's care and blessings, I am cured, I shall come to you personally to greet you and pay homage to you. Whatever I have to say, you know it best and have faith in me, and I request you to favour me by showering your blessings upon me. I am your slave and will live as a slave in the future too. Dr. Moore is present at the hospital. Kindly write to the doctor so that he will give me good medicines necessary for my health. The doctor is going abroad very soon.

ജ

No. 85
17 November 1854

Seal

By name Sindhi *jawan*s, Government employees, year 1854–55, are to be informed that you have been sent to Suddapalle village to collect the due amount, pertaining to the second instalment (land portion) of this revenue year. Now the amount has been received and a little balance remained. Thus, you are relieved now. Report in the office after getting your receipt written, along with the remaining collections.

In connection with the amount from Kurmedu, you wrote that there are no clerks present to deal with. You continued the demand for collections from whoever may be present there, and the property may be kept under attachment.

ജ

No. 86
29 November 1854

Orders of Nawab Salar Jung Bahadur.
To Kishen Rao, *taluqdar*.

It is evident that you have been pressing Raja Rameshwar Rao Balwant Bahiri Bahadur, *zamindar* of the *pargana* of Sugur for the payment of the Government instalment. This is to state that Raja Lakshman Das and Lakshman, bankers, have informed the Government that they are willing to stand surety for the aforesaid Raja. Therefore, you must not press the Raja to pay the arrears. This is a strict Government memo.

☙

No. 87
4 December 1854

Seal

Ghulam Khan.

I am Ghulam Khan, *jamedar*. I have written this in consultation with the Diwan Sahib, Raghuveer Rao, Maharaj. According to the payroll of the Raja Sahib, an amount of Rs 312 and 6 *annas* only is due towards those employees whose services have been terminated. Hence, this is executed as a receipt of disbursement to be used whenever needed.

☙

No. 88
24 December 1854

Gracious Raja Sahib

It is evident from the application submitted by Karim Khan Ghori, *havaldar* of village [illegible], which is the *jagir* of Mir Fida Hussain, that you have been claiming the customary district revenue from the aforesaid *havaldar* for the *pargana* of Sugur and Gopalpet. You are permitted to claim the customary district revenue of the *pargana* of Sugur according to the established tradition. However, as the *rusum* of Gopalpet has now been confiscated by the Government, you are no longer entitled to it and, therefore, must not claim it. This is a strict Government memo.

ꕥ

No. 89
31 December 1854

Gracious Raja Sahib

May you live long. After paying all my humble tributes to you, this is to state that a total amount of Rs 1,500 has been received towards the *rusum* registrar of the *pargana* of Sugur and towards Abi Fasl and Rs 750 towards the *patti* of Aliabad; out of Rs 1,000, Rs 500 has been deducted towards the *patti* of Himkunta and Rs 250 towards Abi Fasl. The remaining amount of Rs 1,000 is sent herewith. Kindly send a receipt for the above-mentioned amount. I am always at the service of the Maharaja.

ꕥ

No. 90
1854–55

Gracious Raja Sahib

From the letters of many *taluqdar*s, it is evident to the Government that *chapatti*s are being sent and distributed in different villages without orders from the Government. However, the name of the person who started this system is not known yet nor has the culprit been traced. If the *taluqdar*s suspected Sahib Bahadur or anybody else, they should have mentioned this in their reports. It is astonishing that the reports sent by some *taluqdar*s do not give details of the happenings in the villages of the *taluq*s. If a suspicious event takes place in any *ilaqa*, it is the duty of the *taluqdar*s, *naib*s and other Government officials of that *ilaqa* to inform the Government, investigate the matter immediately and make arrangements to stop it. It is of no use to send just a formal report or news to the Government if they do not express concern about the matter or take measures to prevent such happenings.

The Government has therefore ordered that enquires be made without leaving a stone unturned in order to find out the name of the village from which the *chapatti*s were sent first as well as the place from which they are being sent at present. The officials must also trace the person who is sending them, state whether the culprit is from within the *ilaqa* of the Government or out of it and his reason for doing this.

The Government employees, *zamindar*s and headmen of their respective *ilaqa*s may also be strictly instructed to make investigations and report back to the Government. The Government would be pleased if early information could be sent on this matter. The persons who are found guilty, irrespective of whether they are headmen or any other person from the village, may be arrested and imprisoned immediately. A list of their names with the nature of their crimes may be sent to the Government so that it can make further investigations and mete out punishments to the offenders. However, while making enquires if it is suspected that the *chapatti*s are being distributed in the name of the Government or Sahib Bahadur, then it is ordered that no action be taken against such persons without strict verification.

The officials are warned that in the future they should be very cautious in all the *ilaqa*s and take notice of every suspicious event. In case of negligence or carelessness on their part towards such acts as this one and the like, firm action will be taken against them and they shall be punished severely.

1855

No. 91
2 January 1855

Draft of the application submitted to Nawab Salar Jung Bahadur.

Your main concern is for the welfare of the people. Nobody would ever dare to act against your wishes no matter how powerful or courageous he may be. Acting on your advice, I have tried to reform myself. I was miserable ever since I was outcasted. I had no future and this had broken my spirit, but by the grace of the Almighty, everybody helped me and guided me. You are the highest authority, and being a conscientious person, you care for the people. You are a man of great wisdom, and you try to show the right path to the people. The common man is born to obey the instructions to him and will not dare to defy them. The *zamindar* of Jatprole has confiscated the village and taken up arms for confrontation by his devious plans. The Government entries have not been made. All this is evident from the *firman* of the ruler. It is learned that you intend to punish the *zamindar*. But now I feel that I have been too impulsive in this regard. I am your old and obedient servant and on whom you bestowed your favours and whom you have restored to dignity. I went to Jatprole along with my troops and confronted the *zamindar*. The *zamindar* arrested me, and after a hunting game, he brought me before you. I may be presented before the ryots and whatever doubts you have about me may be cleared. A notification of my outcasting may be placed before the ryots, and after the agreement of the *zamindar*, action may be taken. You are my master and I shall obey any orders that you issue without any resistance.

ꕥ

No. 92
9 January 1855

Draft of the application to Salar Jung.

Your letter to deduct the customary revenue of village Vespal towards arrears is as usual. In regard to *pargana* Sugur and not necessary for *patti* Gopalpet, it is ordered. I have neither intention nor power to go against the orders. However, you must know the details of this case. Who has the fundamental right of property? My elders were given the right of *watan* of both the *watans*. If you come over here, you may know the truth. My elders are attached always to the court and always favoured by it. Casually if I have not complied with the orders, it was due to my laziness and so for which I have also suffered. Although this slave is deemed criminal in the eyes of the law, you have always pardoned it and appointed me on the same post because from a very long period I am by you.

[In verse] 'To separate the wood from water, I know not what secret it had; I feel ashamed to be fed by my relatives.'

Therefore, I request that I may be allowed to file a counter for both the *rusums*. I, the humble servant, am ever-obedient and prepared to serve, and hope that you would issue orders to the *havaldar* of the both villages to issue the *rusum* so that I may pray day and night for your prosperity.

ഇ

No. 93
2 May 1855

Gracious Raja Sahib

The reply to the application that you had submitted to the Government has been received. The letter sent by the Resident is enclosed herewith.

ഇ

No. 94
15 May 1855

Umdat-ul-Mulk to Manjle Miyan

To the Honourable Princess

It has been learnt that you are not keeping well these days. We are your humble servants and are praying to God day and night for your health. Kindly inform me as soon as you recover. I pray to God for your health.

ഇ

No. 95
15 May 1855

Dear Jamedar Sahib

My salutation to you. This is to state that you had not informed your well-wisher about your health and well-being for a long time. After a gap of over a month, I was happy to receive your letter. I remain eager to see you.

ꕥ

No. 96
11 June 1855

Honourable Resident Bahadur

After my humble salutations, I have to state that I am working under Muhiddin, resident of Pagtoor. From the day of my entering service till this day, salary of eight months is held by Sibghatullah Khan, *jamedar*. It is for your knowledge that I have never come for leave of at least a week to think that due to it the *jamedar* has withheld it. I live at the village Yaparla. If it is ordered, I shall go there and claim my salary. Until this total period, I have availed only one day's leave. I am financially hard-pressed. I have sent the clerk and Muhuddin Sahib; you may kindly ask them and confirm it.

ꕥ

No. 97
25 June 1855

Seal
Nawab Imad-ul-Mulk Bahadur
Zainul Abidin Khan
Ahmed Yar Jung Bahadur.

Dear Naib Sahib

With love and affection. It has come to the knowledge of the Government that Topnath Naganna, resident of the village of Rajpal in the *pargana* of Kundurg, owes Rs 12,000 to the moneylender Mallaiah of Bakshi Gunj Bazaar in the *ilaqa* of the Nawab Sahib. However, the Mallaiah's brother agreed to accept Rs 6,000 only. Topath Naganna has not repaid the above-said amount yet. Hence, this is to request that as soon as you receive this letter, send Topath Naganna to this place so that he may be presented in the Government office. Moreover, a copy of the orders of the Raja is also enclosed herewith. Kindly go through it and give your opinion about it herewith in a few lines, because a letter would almost be like meeting. For the rest, all is well.

ꙮ

No. 98
24 August 1855

To the agents, record keepers, *havaldar*s, agents of the *maniwar*s, headmen, accountants, ryots and the cultivators of the *mazra*s of *pargana* Sugur and Kothakota, *sarkar* Pangal, *patti* of Molgara, *pargana* of Godal, *patti* of Taru, *pargana* of Amrabad, *patti* of Kesampeta, *pargana* of Cherikonda and *jagir*s in the *pargana* of Avancha.

The above-said *pargana* from the beginning of the year 1855–56 has been entrusted to Babuji Seth. Now the aforesaid Seth may take possession of the *pargana* and consider himself permanent. He must improve the cultivation and pay the fixed and proper revenue on time to the Government. This *sanad* may be considered reliable.

[Signed] Muhammad

ꙮ

No. 99
15 October 1855

Seal

By the name of Devarakonda Venkata Ramaiah, fixed rate holder, village Suddapalle, this is to inform that while writing a long letter, you have stated that Narayana Rao of Kesampeta jurisdiction has prevented you from paying the second instalment (land portion) of revenue, pertaining to the aforesaid village for the year 1855–56, stating that the amount should not be remitted here at our place. As you know the Government revenue is being remitted here, year by year, since a long time. Now you write that they have prevented you from paying the revenue to us. It seems to be improper. Hence, the same may be arranged soon and be remitted to us immediately. A peon is also going to be deputed from here for this purpose.

ꕥ

No. 100
1855

Gracious Raja Sahib

Your letter sent by the peon on 13 May 1855 has been received and I learnt about the state of affairs. You have mentioned in your letter that you are going to see Captain Jackson Bahadur regarding some cases. In that case, it would be appropriate if I came there after a day or two. Kind sir, today is Sunday, and a holiday for the aforesaid Bahadur since he is a Christian. Perhaps you are there now. It is better to straighten out the affairs with the Government. I am well. I am deeply attached to you and your company gives me pleasure. I shall be at your service in times of need.

ꕥ

No. 101
1855–56

Raja Chandu Lal Bahadur

Gracious Raja Sahib

I have come to know through Sachanand Swami that the agreement between you and the Government has already been formalised in writing. Consequently, it is necessary that you must act according to the agreement, but it is learnt that you have often exceeded your limits. Complaints have reached the Maharaja that you have forcefully taken away the cattle from the ryots and are harassing and troubling them. This is to remind you that according to the agreement, you had promised to maintain peace and treat the ryots well. It is evident that you have not kept your promise, but if you do not restrain yourself from such activities, the Government shall be compelled to take action against you. Hence, this is written to you in a friendly spirit. The rest is up to you. However, you must not lay your hands on Sanjiv Rao and Sulemandar because according to the agreement they have paid the amount to Dasappa Naik.

ꕥ

No. 102
1855–56

I begin with the name of Allah who is the most merciful.

Allah who loves those who are most generous. The question of Haji Abdur Rahim who had come here to earn his living and now intends to go back to his own country. Yet, he is helpless owing to his condition. If you wish to donate to charity, kindly give it to him in the name of Allah. On reaching his country, he will pray to God for your health and prosperity.

ꕥ

No. 103
1855–56

Seal: rectangular
Rajayan-e-raja/ Raja-e-rajayan
Raja Chandu Lal Bahadur

Gracious Raja Sahib

From a letter written by your agent, Ranga Reddi, it is learnt that Narsimha Reddi, *deshmukh* of the *pargana* of Yeljal, has taken to stealing. As soon as you have proof of this, the aforesaid must be arrested and brought to the office of the Government.

ꕥ

No. 104
1855–56

Gracious Raja Sahib

It is learnt through the Honourable Resident Bahadur that the *deshmukh* of Naikra Rajapur, which is located in the vicinity of Kondanagula, is proving to be troublesome. He has engaged some Rohillas, etc., in his *ilaqa* to plunder the *ilaqa* of the English. Hence, this is to state that you must send your troops in the concerned *ilaqa* to arrest the aforesaid and punish him accordingly.

ぎ

No. 105
1855–56

Seal
Hashmat Jung Fidvi of Munir Izad Yar Khan Asaf Jah Bahadur

Smt. Janaki Zamindarni

Pargana Sugur.

Madam Bhat, your *vakil* approached the court and was greeted. He has corrected some affairs of your estate. Whatever promises you have made in the Government, the faith is in its completion to please the Government. The rest is in person.

ぎ

No. 106
1855–56

Almighty.

To Your Exalted Highness

After my salutations, this is to state that we are always praying to God for your welfare. This is to inform you that any family of six, including children and adults, has to spend days in starvation and is under pressure from the moneylenders. In such conditions, it is too difficult for me to eat. In the first place I am under pressure from the moneylenders. Secondly, I can no more think of a way of providing my family with food. I am helpless and have no means of support. For this reason, I have submitted an application and I request you to kindly take care of my life and relieve me of the pressure from the moneylenders. [In verse] 'The heart of this injured has turned towards you.' As for the rest, you are my master.

[Signed] Abdur Rasul Khan Lohani

ꟸ

No. 107
1855–56

Gracious Raja Sahib

According to the orders of the Honourable Resident Bahadur, Mr. Smith [illegible] is being exiled from the precincts of the Government. Therefore, you must send him out of the Government boundaries.

1856

No. 108
22 January 1856

Gracious Raja Sahib

From the letter of the Resident Bahadur, it is evident that the Raja of *samasthan* Shorapur has recruited a troop of Rohillas and Arabs with the intention of rebellion, although he himself is held captive by his own troops. A troop is being sent by the Government to punish him. This is to state that on receipt of this order, you must immediately make arrangements at the *ghat*s and the outposts of your *ilaqa* so that no one is allowed to cross the borders of this province. If they do not turn back in spite of your orders, they may be arrested immediately. If the people of your *ilaqa* go individually or in groups to that place, they may be asked to return. If they refuse, they may be punished. This is a strict Government memo.

ꙮ

No. 109
31 July 1856

Gracious Raja Sahib

The Government has learnt that you have pulled down the houses in the areas of Gar'i, Wanaparthy and Sugur, and that the wood of those houses has already been used to construct a beautiful house. This act of yours has displeased the Government. Although you are forgiven this time, it is ordered that in the future you must be careful that such acts are not repeated.

ꙮ

No. 110
25 December 1856

Seal
Niyabat-e-diwani.

To the *taluqdar*s, *naib*s, *zamindar*s, etc., of the *taluq* of the Government.

Messrs Burhanuddin and Badruddin, *ilaqadar*s under the *maniwari* of the *pargana* of Sugur have wounded and killed some farmers, and then fled. You must search for them in your *ilaqa*s, and wherever they are found, they may be arrested and sent with an escort to the *taluqdar* of Sugur or to the office of the Government. It may be announced in your *ilaqa*s that the Government has offered a reward of Rs 100 to whoever provides clues as to the whereabouts of the aforesaid and helps in arresting them.

ꙮ

No. 111
1856–57

Seal: rectangular

Gracious Raja Sahib

You are a well-wisher of the Government, but I am amazed that the *naib* of your *ilaqa* has developed a grudge against the grain merchants because they did not provide conveyance to your *naib*s nor did they pay *nazrana* to them. To punish the grain merchants, the *naib* is trying to destroy the *taluq*. The watchmen, too, have not remained loyal and are plundering the *taluq*. The *maniwar* is answerable for the thefts and dacoities in his area. Therefore, you must purify your inner self, and without any grudges, you must make proper arrangements for the protection of your ryots. To take revenge on the poor people is unfair, and such acts should not be supported. Therefore, you must instruct the watchmen to perform their duties properly and work together with the above-said *naib* to protect the people against robberies.

ཐ

No. 112
1856–57

Gracious Raja Sahib

From your letter to the members of the Majlis, it is evident that you thought Shayar-ul-Mulk Bahadur had received the amount of Rs 1,000 that was due to Muhammad Ali, *hundikar*, a resident of Bombay from Sangam *zamindar*. Thus, the aforesaid *zamindar* who had been sent to you earlier was thought to be innocent and was released. But the above-cited amount has not been received by the Bahadur. Therefore, it is necessary that the *zamindar* be arrested again and brought before the Government. It was not a wise act to have released the *zamindar* without the knowledge of the Government. Mutahhawar Jung's son informed that you went to the *taluq* of Tandur and arrested the *zamindar* and the thieves with cash. The *hundikar* has stated that he has lost articles worth Rs 2,653 and has filed a claim for these articles. Where are the other stolen valuables? Some of the stolen articles are with you; therefore, the responsibility for recovering the other goods of the *hundikar* also rests with you. You must send a report of this matter to the Government immediately.

ꟸ

No. 113
1856–57

Seal: rectangular
Mukhtar-ul-Mulk

Gracious Raja Sahib

From the letter of Munsir Jung, *taluqdar* of Gulbarga, it is evident that Basant Singh, an Asami from Shorapur, and his associates were arrested by the constables of the above-mentioned *taluqdar*, and their statements have been taken. Captain Young has ordered the *taluqdar* to hand these people over to him. This is against the rules, and Captain Young's interference in this matter is disapproved of. For this reason, these cases were submitted to the office of the Government in consultation with the Majlis. Hence, your attitude in this regard is wrong.

You know well that the miscreants who are in the aforesaid *taluqdar*'s custody can at present not be handed over to Captain Young. On the contrary, after due investigation into such cases, a *taluqdar* has to submit his report to the Government. The main duty of the troops stationed in the districts is to trace the robbers and dacoits, and to attack them without warning. After arresting them, they are handed over to the *taluqdar*, who, according to the orders sent by the Government, will either bring them to a court of law or send them wherever required. A *ziladar* may not ask for the people arrested by a *taluqdar*. In the future, you must be careful about this.

No. 114
1856–57

Gracious Raja Sahib

It is learnt that Paras Ram Reddi, the *zamindar* of the *taluq* of Ghanapur, has mischievously injured the ryots of the village [illegible] and taken away the belongings and cattle from the people. Hence, the ryots lodged a complaint against him with the Government. Therefore, it is ordered that the cattle and belongings of the ryots be taken back from the aforesaid *deshmukh* and returned to the ryots. It must be taken in writing from the *zamindar* that he will not repeat such an act in the future, failing which he will be punished.

No. 115
1856–57

Gracious Raja Sahib

An application from Syed Dastagir Qadri, a resident of Kurnool, has been received in which he has stated that the money and other belongings of the *mashaikh*s of Kurnool and Alampur were looted at Bhuthpur when they were returning to their native land, and that they had been wounded by the robbers. It is ordered that since you are the *maniwar* of Bhuthpur, you must arrest the robbers and recover the articles from them. The articles must be returned to the owners, and the robbers must be punished so that they do not indulge in such acts again.

No. 116
1856–57

Gracious Raja Sahib

Sri Haji Muhammad Ibn Ibrahim Abdullah Rumi, the murderer of Sri Govind Ram Marwadi, has absconded. A description of the aforesaid is enclosed herewith. It is ordered that the murderer, wherever he is found in your territory, be arrested and sent along with a proper escort to the Government. A notice may be printed announcing that whoever arrests the previously mentioned individual will be paid a sum of Rs 500 by the Government.

ꟈ

No. 117
1856–57

Gracious Raja Sahib

The real name of Sri Sarfaraz Husain who was appointed *tehsildar* of Kuppal is Zahur Hussain. In view of the seriousness of his crime, a troop from Lingasur cantonment is being sent to arrest him according to the orders of the Government. On hearing this news, the aforesaid has fled on horseback. The above-mentioned is young, his complexion is wheat-coloured and he has a black spot below the right eye. Wajihuddin Khan, the second *taluqdar* of Kuppal, has written to the other *taluqdar*s of that area regarding his arrest. It is now stated that you must conduct a search for him in your *ilaqa*, and if you arrest him, he must be sent with an escort to the Government.

ꟈ

No. 118
1856–57

Gracious Raja Sahib

From the letter of the Honourable Resident Bahadur, it has been learnt that ninety-four lancers, fifty-five cannoneers, 600 people belonging to the 59th battalion and thirty-five other persons will be reaching the banks of the Krishna River on 3 December 1857 on their way to Secunderabad. Therefore, you must supply them with the required provisions, and make every effort to ensure that no complaints reach here.

ꟈ

No. 119
1856–57

The order has been sanctioned to you. You must be satisfied and win the confidence of the old and the new ryots, improve the cultivation, rehabilitate the village and pay the fixed amount to the Government according to the instalments. You must not have any doubt, but be satisfied. This is an order.

1857

No. 120
2 May 1857

Nawab Salar Jung Bahadur
Seal: rectangular
Krishna Rao

A copy of the receipt having the signature and the seal of the Nawab Sahib has been received. May his stars always be in the ascendant.

Rai Venkat Krishna Reddi, the adopted son of Rai Rangai, wife of the late Subba Reddi, *deshmukh*, has sent an amount of Rs 4,000 (the half of which amounts to Rs 2,000) in consultation with Subba Rao to restore the *watan deshmukhi* and *nar'gauri* of the *patti* of Rachala, *pargana* of Kandur alias Devarkadra, *sarkar* Ghanapur, *subah* Farkhunda Bunyad, Hyderabad, in accordance with the traditions since 1856–57. The above-mentioned amount has been submitted in the office of the Government.

ꟻ

No. 121
12 May 1857

Seal: rectangular
Salar Jung Bahadur

Rai Venkat Krishna Reddi [illegible] Rai Venkai, wife of the late Subba Reddi, *deshmukh*, has sent an amount of Rs 4,000 (the half of which amounts to Rs 2,000) in consultation with Kishan Rao towards the *watan deshmukhi* and *nar'gauri* of the *patti* of Rachala, *pargana* of Kandur alias Devarkadra, *sarkar* Ghanapur, *subah* Farkhunda Bunyad, Hyderabad. This amount was due since the beginning of the year 1856–57. It must be submitted in the office of the Government.

ΩЗ

No. 122
12 May 1857

Nawab Salar Jung Bahadur
Seal: square

Received a copy having the signature and seal of the Nawab Sahib. May God bring him prosperity.

Rai Venkat Krishan Reddi, the adopted son of Rai Rangai, wife of the late Subba Reddi, *deshmukh*, has sent an amount of Rs 4,000 (the half of which amounts to Rs 2,000) in consultation with Kishan Rao to restore the *watan deshmukhi* and *nar'gauri* of the *patti* of Rachala *pargana* of Kandur alias Devarkadra, *sarkar* Ghanapur, *subah* Farkhunda Bunyad, Hyderabad during 1856–57. The above-mentioned amount has been submitted in the office of the Government.

ΩЗ

No. 123
12 June 1857

Nawab Salar Jung Bahadur.

A copy of the Government orders under the signature and seal of the Nawab Sahib, addressed to Krishna Rao *taluqdar*.

In accordance with the tradition the *watan deshmukhi* and *nar'gauri* of the *patti* of Rachala, *pargana* of Kandur alias Devarkadra, *sarkar* Ghanapur, *subah* Farkhunda Bunyad, Hyderabad has been restored to Rai Venkat Krishna Reddi, *deshmukh*, the adopted son of Rai Rangai, wife of the late Subba Reddi Deshmukh, in 1856–57. Therefore, the salary, *rusum*, other sources of revenue along with necessaries, dependencies, signatures and *man-o-pan*, etc., also may be granted to him as is customary. This is an order.

ꙮ

No. 124
12 August 1857

I, Sawai Raja Rameshwar Rao Bahiri Balwant Bahadur, do hereby state that I have taken the *pargana* of Sugur and Kothakota in *sarkar* Pangal, *subah* Farkhunda Bunyad, Hyderabad, on the stipulated fixed rate for an amount of Rs 77,006, from the beginning of the year 1857–58 till the end of 1861–62, i.e., for a period of five years. Govind Naik, the moneylender, will stand surety for me. I agree to pay the amount yearly according to the instalments fixed; as for the other amount which I have to pay, I will credit it to the Government treasury with the consent of the above-mentioned moneylender, and obtain a receipt for it. I will rehabilitate the *taluq* and keep the ryots happy and satisfied. I will also make the necessary arrangements in the *taluq* to safeguard it against theft. I will make efforts to arrest the thieves, recover the stolen articles and hand them over to the authority concerned. I will also make arrangements for the safety of the highway and will not join in any troublesome activities. Whenever ordered by the Government, I will appear before the Royal Court. If I fail to comply with any of the assurances that I have given in this document, I may be considered worthy of blame. I will willingly accept any punishment that the Government wishes to mete out to me.

In case I am unable to pay the amount and the arrears to the Government one time, I request that fifteen days grace be given to me. If I fail to pay it before the expiry of the period, then the Government, in consultation with the moneylender, may impose whatever fines it desires and may also take back the management of the above-mentioned *taluq*. In such a case, I would have no cause for complaint. Thus I have written these few words in agreement and acceptance.

Khilat Rs 3,540
Salary of the agent Rs 490
Expenses towards the food for the elephant Rs 730
Daily allowance given Rs 3,006

ꙮ

No. 125
19 September 1857

Seal: rectangular
Salar Jung

Gracious Raja Sahib

It has come to my knowledge that a person named Chinna Erkalla who was married to the daughter of Napar Muttiga died leaving a wife and a daughter. After his death, his wife took her daughter and went to stay in her father's house. Taking all the belongings, cattle, the wife and daughter of the deceased with him, Muttiga, migrated to the village of Gorwaram in the *ilaqa* of Wanaparthy and has been living there in peace since then. Some people like Pilbai Ganga, etc., approached the *panchayat* of their caste. Muttiga learnt that Pilbai Ganga has accused him of stealing cattle. Hence, this is to state that Muttiga must await the decision that shall be taken after an enquiry is made.

No. 126
6 November 1857

Seal: rectangular
Mukhtar-ul-Mulk

Gracious Raja Sahib

An amount of Rs 1,500, salary *rusum* and other sources of revenue, registrar of the *pargana* Sugur and Kothakota in the *ilaqa* of Raja Ram Prashad Lala Bahadur, for the year 1857–58 according to customary payment, this has been given to your agent. A receipt for the same has been obtained. The record keeper's signature, register, *man-o-pan*, and dependencies and hereditary right have also been issued. This is a Government memo.

ഌ

No. 127
1857

Seal: rectangular
Mukhtar-ul-Mulk

Gracious Raja Sahib

From a letter of the Honourable Resident Bahadur, it is learnt that the 43rd regiment of soldiers comprising thirty officers (sergeants), 938 soldiers, seven elephants, forty-eight camels, and 2,000 people of the bazaar; the 19th platoon with seventy officers, twenty ranking officers, fifty *havaldars*, 670 sepoys and 1,000 people of the bazaar; and a troop of the 50th regiment, i.e., 125 sepoys and 100 people of the bazaar will reach Kyatur on 22 January 1858. From here, they will proceed to Bawan via Bikkam. When these people reach your territory, provisions must be supplied to them at cost price. It is learnt through the commander that the people of the villages sell articles at very high prices to the army people. Therefore, you must warn them strictly that they must charge only the cost price. Care must be taken to see that no one charges extra. If any person is found to be charging in excess of the regular price, the Government will prosecute him. This is an order and must be complied with.

1858 

No. 128
25 January 1858

Seal

By name Gurunam Singh under the jurisdiction of Nizamath, year 1857–58, is informed that you have been sent to Suddapalle village for the amounts to be collected there; now you are being relieved. Hence, have your receipt written and come back.

༺

No. 129
10 February 1858

Seal: round
Niyabad-e-diwani
Nizam-ul-Mulk Asaf Jah Bahadur

To the agents of the *jagirdars*, *faujdars*, *maniwars*, *chaukidars*, *rahdaran* and to all passersby of the highways.

Sawai Raja Rameshwar Rao Balwant Bahiri Bahadur is appointed by the Government to make arrangements at the outposts of the boundaries with Shorapur with troops of footmen and horsemen from Humnabad, Farooqnagar, Jadcherla, Bhuthpur, Janumpet and Makhtal. You may supply the provisions and hay to the Raja Sahib. However, you must purchase them and hand them over to the Raja Sahib in the presence of a Government attendant, thereby leaving no scope for mismanagement. You may also appoint begars at the above-mentioned route to let the Raja Sahib pass without any obstruction. This is a Government order.

No. 130
22 March 1858

Gracious Raja Sahib

From the application of Kanda Swami, it is evident that two or three houses of other ryots in the village of Yenacherla have also been robbed besides his own. The post of *maniwar* of that village has been assigned to you. Therefore, this is to state that as soon as you receive this order, you must make enquiries and try to trace the robbers. You must arrest them, and recover the stolen articles from them and return them to their owners. This is a strict Government memo.

ꕤ

No. 131
15 January 1858

Seal: rectangular
Mukhtar-ul-Mulk

Respected Sir

A letter written by you earlier binding the *naib*s of the *taluq* of Sugur of Raja Rameshwar Rao Bahadur, *zamindar*, not to interfere in the contracts of the above-mentioned *pargana* has been received. The revenue of the above-said *pargana* has been fixed in consultation with Govind Naik, moneylender. The aforesaid Bahadur has also sent his agreement and the salary of the employees, etc., of the above-said *pargana* to the Government with the consent of the above-said moneylender. Therefore, you may post one clerk along with ten people of your *ilaqa* in the above city *pargana* only to observe and report back to you, and not to interfere in the contract and *tehsil* work of the *pargana*.

ꕤ

No. 132
11 February 1858

Gracious Raja Sahib

An amount of Rs 2,378 for the troops and your escort has been appointed recently for the settlement of the *ghat*s and outposts on the boundary of Shorapur. Therefore, you must now draw the above-mentioned amount and take Rs 1,500 out of it. You must spend the remaining amount on the troops. The details of such disbursements and the receipts for the same should be submitted in the office of the Government. The gunpowder required should be purchased from the amount of the tehsil of the above-mentioned *pargana*.

No. 133
2 April 1858

Seal: rectangular
Mukhtar-ul-Mulk

Gracious Raja Sahib

From a petition sent to the Government by Govind Rao, the *taluqdar* of Medak, it is evident that bullocks were purchased by one of the ryots named Chinnaiah. However, while changing his house, he took away all his belongings to the village of Wasil in the *pargana* of Avancha. As the district revenue of that area has been assigned to you, it is your responsibility to trace the thief. However, in spite of not having attended to the duties required of him, Uma Rao, your agent, has staked a claim to the customary district revenue. Therefore, it is ordered that Uma Rao must make whole-hearted efforts to apprehend the thief, and only after that is accomplished, may he claim the customary district revenue.

No. 134
30 April 1858

This is an application from Syed Dastagir Qadri in which he says that a group of twenty people, including women, while travelling on Friday, the new moon of Ramzan, were attacked by robbers at Bhuthpur, which is in the *ilaqa* district revenue of Raja Rameshwar Rao. In the ensuing scuffle, the writer was wounded. The robbers looted the money and other items belonging to the caravan. A list of the looted articles has been submitted by Dastagir Qadri, who has requested the Government to write to the Raja Sahib for their recovery.

ꙮ

No. 135
17 May 1858

Gracious Raja Sahib

On 2 April of this year, a letter was written to your agent, Appa Rao, binding him to obtain the description of the people who had plundered the belongings and goods from the house of Vassal Chinnaiah, resident of the village of Vassal. Only then can he claim the customary district revenue. Although the above-cited orders were issued in his name, he has not complied with them yet. Keeping the Government orders pending for so long is not proper. The aforesaid agent is adamant and has staked a claim to the customary district revenue before attending to the duty required of him. Therefore, this is to state that as soon as you receive this order, the agent may be warned and bound not to claim the *rusum* till he sends us the information about the people who plundered the village. This is a strict Government memo.

ꙮ

No. 136
26 May 1858

Seal: rectangular
Mukhtar-ul-Mulk

Gracious Raja Sahib

It is learnt that when Maulvi Sibghatullah, *ilaqadar* of the Adalat was journeying towards Kurnool, thieves looted some money and belongings worth about Rs 200 from him at Bhuthpur. It is possible that the thieves may be from the same place. As the district revenue of the village adjacent to Bhuthpur has been assigned to you, it is necessary that you trace the thieves, arrest them with the stolen articles and bring them before the Government. This is an order and must be complied with.

ꕤ

No. 137
22 June 1858

Seal: round
Niyabat-e-diwani
Nizam-ul-Mulk Asaf Jah Bahadur.

Order of permission to travel.

To the agents of the *jagirdar*s, *faujdar*s, *maniwar*s, *chaukidar*s, and all those who guard the outposts and the highways.

Sawai Raja Rameshwar Rao Balwant Bahiri Bahadur has been appointed to make arrangements at the police stations and *ghat*s, etc., on the boundary of Kuppal Bahadur Banda. Hence, he will go there along with his troops of 100 cavalry. Therefore, when he reaches your *ilaqa* you should supply grains, hay and other necessary commodities to him on a settled price in the presence of the staff bearer, and escort him safely through your *ilaqa*. This is a strict order and must be complied with.

ꕤ

No. 138
5 July 1858

Sri Bawa Sahib, a resident of Wanaparthy, has stolen four cows from my house and taken them from there. I humbly request you to issue an order to Sawai Raja Rameshwar Rao Balwant Bahiri Bahadur to help me in getting back my cows. I am poor and entirely depend on those cows for my livelihood.

Petitioner, Muhammad Iqbal.
Resident of Janumpet.

ဢ

No. 139
6 July 1858

Seal: rectangular
Mukhtar-ul-Mulk

Gracious Raja Sahib

Muhammad Iqbal, resident of Janumpet, has submitted an application stating that four cows have been stolen from his house. Hence, this is to state that you may make an enquiry about the theft and recover the cows, so that they may be handed over to the owner. This is a strict Government memo.

ဢ

No. 140
27 July 1858

Seal: rectangular
Mukhtar-ul-Mulk

Gracious Raja Sahib

From the application of Bazaid Khan, it is evident that a person named Mayana has broken the boat of Govind Naik, a resident of the village of

Yaparla, *taluq* of Sugur, *ghat* fort Pagtur, and used the planks and iron for the construction of a temple. It has been stated that Govind Naik had left his boat at the *ghat*, fort Pagtur. You may kindly ascertain the facts and inform the Government.

℘

No. 141
28 July 1858

Gracious Raja Sahib

Kankai Janai, *deshmukhni* of *patti* Taduru in *pargana* Amrabad, which is in the *ilaqa* of Muhammad Budhan Khan Bahadur, refused to hand over the possession of the above-mentioned *patti* and its finances. Moreover, she has been taking favours from you, and despite this, she has not been paying the revenue tax of Sangavaram village, etc., and of the surrounding fixed rate lands within that village. Hence, Balav Rao submitted a draft pertaining to this matter, a copy of which is enclosed and which may kindly be returned after a detailed report about the reasons for the state of affairs mentioned is sent to the Government.

℘

No. 142
1 August 1858

Seal: rectangular
Mukhtar-ul-Mulk

Gracious Raja Sahib

From the application of Kishan Rao, *taluqdar* of the Government, it is learnt that you have written a rather rude letter to him. You have not only omitted his titles, etc., but also sounded as though you were giving orders to him. This is not appropriate and is against the custom. Hence, this is to state that in the future you must respect the dignity of the Government servants and write to them keeping their prestige in view.

℘

No. 143
8 August 1858

On 15 September 1857, orders were issued to you regarding the retrieval of stolen goods from the house of Ramaiah, *kulkarni*, and Sujju Rao, headman of the village of Chigur, *pargana* of Nar'khora, which are kept in custody of Kanda Swami, *taluqdar* of the Government. You were ordered to bring the thieves to the office of the Government or to compensate them for the stolen goods in case you failed to recover them. From the report of the aforesaid *taluqdar* it is learnt that instead of carrying out the orders yourself, you had made your *naib* Kunda Reddi, *maniwar*, responsible for making arrangements to arrest the thieves with the stolen goods or to compensate the loss. A few days later, you wrote to the above-said *naib* and signed an agreement according to which you would carry out the orders yourself. However, you have not acted according to it until now, which is deplorable. The aforesaid *taluqdar* sent a few horsemen and *jawans* to the above-cited village to collect the *rusum maniwar* from the village in order to compensate the loss. They arrested the liquor merchants of both villages and tortured them to collect the *rusum* from them. This is wrong. Hence, this is to state that as soon as you receive this order you must release the liquor merchants and inform the Government. In case you have taken anything from them, either in cash or in kind, you may return it to them, and obtain a receipt for the same. This is a strict Government memo.

1859

No. 144
1859–60

Gracious Raja Sahib

Taluq Makhtal, etc., had been given in custody of Mirza Muhsin, by hearing this you have suspended Naga Rao, Amil in village Kandur, and kept the outpost Swaipally under you. It is necessary for the Raja to establish outposts in other *taluqs*. It is also better for you. The other Asamis of *pargana* Kundur are arrested, punished and kept in your prison; the ryot of that *pargana* is confounded. You have kept Bukai, wife of late Juka Reddi, under your protection, and on behalf of her, you are doing her work. Hence, it is to state that you must refrain from such acts, and going to the village may be restored and the anxiety of the Asamis may be relaxed. The details of the Asamis are enclosed, and in near future, Mirza Muhsin shall be sent to that side.

ꟿ

No. 145
1859–60

Gracious Raja Sahib

Your letter has been received. According to your request, orders governed by the Muslim Law have been issued in the name of Ghulam Qadir Khan, Qadi Jatprole, who awaits the judgment of murder of Jan Muhammad Khan Bilouch (and referred to as Hasanuddin Khan). This is a Government memo.

ꟿ

No. 146
1859–60

Gracious Raja Sahib

The generous and kind court has accorded permission to Sawai Raja Ram Krishna Rao Bahadur, *deshmukh* of *pargana* Sugur, for minting the coins of Sugur. It is necessary that the deputy of the villages and the *parganas* may prepare them according to those weights adopted in Gadwal and Narayanpet, and regulate them at the *taluqs* and the villages of your estate. This is a strict Government memo.

ꟿ

No. 147
1859–60

Gracious Raja Sahib

A copy of the order from the Adalat-ul-Aliya (higher court) may be sent to the Munsif and another copy of the same with the original order to the Government. This is a Government memo.

ꕥ

No. 148
1859–60

Gracious Raja Sahib

On investigation into the cases of theft and dacoity on the highways of Bhongir, Malkapur, Ibrahimpatnam, Mallepalle, Nalgonda, etc., it has been determined that the dacoits are being aided by three liquor merchants and the village headmen and accountants of Mallepalle village. Captain Malcolm, who was sent by the Resident Bahadur to conduct the investigation, has informed the Government that a gang of thieves is residing on the entire lands of the said village in *taluq* Bhongir, with the knowledge of the village headmen of that place. After committing the thefts on the highway, the thieves came south, towards Bhongir and the Krishna River. Many of them are Banjaras and Telangas, from the surrounding places of Wanaparthy, Ibrahimpatnam, Mallepalle and Malkapur. They arrived in Lolepally after looting the travellers on the highway. If any person offered resistance, he was killed. This must be stopped. Hence, it is ordered that you must adopt effective measures to prevent the Banjaras living in the troop on that side from leaving. Anyone resembling a Banjara in face or dress must not be allowed to cross to the other side of the river. If, however, a person does leave the troop, enquiries must be made as to where he is going and for what purpose he left the troop. These arrangements are necessary because these people are the suspected thieves. If you can get a witness to testify against them, they may be arrested. But you will have to take the responsibility for such an action. Treat this as a warning.

ꕥ

No. 149
1859–60

From the letter of the Magistrate of Kurnool, which was sent to the Honourable Resident Bahadur, it is learnt that a mob of about 300 Rohillas plundered village Kothakota, *taluq* Dopath, and killed one horseman while wounding another. After stealing a horse on 4 February of the present year, they have absconded from there. The list of looted articles and the description of the stolen horses is enclosed. You are requested that a thorough search for the Rohillas be made in your territory and a report of the same may be sent to the Government. This is a Government memo.

ꕥ

No. 150
1859–60

Seal: rectangular
Shams-ul-Mulk

Gracious Raja Sahib

The petitioner with the opinion of Raghubar Rao, representative, came here with one *mohur ashrafi* and Rs 5 as a *nazrana*, and he was presented before the Nizam. Whatever request he had with him was read in detail. Now the Government must know the actual position and decide on forwarding the requests.

ꕥ

No. 151
1859–60

Seal: rectangular
Mansoor-ud-Daula

Respected Rani Sahiba

My sons Syed Fateh Ali Khan and Syed Ibrahim Ali Khan with their dependants are going to Hyderabad. For this you may provide your forces to escort them till the end of your territory. With best compliments.

☙

No. 152
1859–60

Gracious Raja Sahib

It has come to the notice that you have adopted the activities of devastation and are using force. By your activities, it is also evident that you have become disobedient to the Government, hence, it is said that you may be brought under discipline by the Government troops. The intention here is that first it may be enquired of you in this regard so that you may reply, in person, the correct interpretation for your above activities. Therefore, it is to state that without any pause, you should come to Hyderabad; bringing any armed people with you is not good and it would be irritating. Hence, you may bring a few people in your retinue who are essential to serve you. One road tax permit is enclosed with it. On the way to Hyderabad, nobody should obstruct you. It is hoped that you would immediately proceed without any pause. In case of non-compliance by you, it is necessary that force may be sent against you. You must refrain from such things for the favours of the court. You may not separate yourself from the court. The ruler would take steps against the traitors. In regard to you, they would adopt the procedure that they deem fit.

☙

No. 153
1859–60

Gracious Raja Sahib

A memo was issued on the 4th of this month regarding the arrest of a person who calls himself both Raghunath Rao and Kishan Rao. As suggested by his associate, Kalidas Gujarati, his description is enclosed herewith. He is travelling alone and moving around from place to place. Government troops have been sent out in different directions around the capital for his arrest. Therefore, this is to order you again to search for the aforesaid, and arrest him with the help of the other *zamindar*s and *maniwar*s. In this case, you may not work in secret. In case you are found not searching and arresting of the aforesaid, the Government would prosecute you.

ꓭ

No. 154
1859–60

Gracious Raja Sahib

From a letter written by Captain Byler, which was sent here by the Honourable Resident Bahadur, it is evident that a Government troop has been posted in your *ilaqa* to arrest the miscreants who were associated with the revolt at Shorapur. In order to arrest Siddi Nasib, the troop chased him as far as Nanded, but the *naib* of that town (who is an Arab) and the other Arabs refused to hand him over. Therefore, you are ordered to send a detailed report stating the number of people who chased him, under whose command they were and the name of the Naib of Nanded. Who those Arabs are and what reason they have given for protecting the Siddi may also be written so that the Government may investigate the matter fully.

ꓭ

No. 155
1859–60

Gracious Raja Sahib

The Honourable Resident Bahadur has informed us that Arif Ali, Siddi Suleman and one other person, who were arrested at Pargi for having participated in the Shorapur revolt, are being sent from there to Captain Taylor at Shorapur. Since you have appointed Yenkiah to lead the troop sent out to search for and arrest the rebels of Shorapur, you may write to him, with the order that he should reach Pargi without delay along with a large troop. Or you may send any other trusted person with a letter to the *naib* of that place, asking him to take the aforesaid three persons into his custody. Taking due precautions, they may be sent to the above-mentioned Captain at Shorapur. If any of the prisoners escape, you will be held responsible. This is a strict Government order.

ꕤ

No. 156
1859–60

Gracious Raja Sahib

The Government does not approve of giving *taluq* divisions, villages on lease or *sarbasta*s to strange Marathas or suspected people. Therefore, this is to state that you may prepare a list of people who at present are lease holders or contractors in your *ilaqa*, giving details such as name, place of residence, post held and the name of the *ilaqa*. It should also be stated whether he is a lease holder or a subsidised farmer, what the total period of his contract is, how much of this has elapsed and how much is remaining. This is to be reported immediately so that if further applications are received for leases or at subsidised rent, the *watandar*s may be preferred in whom the Government has full confidence. However, they must not have links of any kind with the mischievous and unsocial elements.

ꕤ

No. 157
1859–60

Gracious Raja Sahib

It has come to the notice of the Government that the *taluqdar*s, *naib*s and other employees of the *taluq*s have been purchasing grain and cotton from the people, and are reselling it for a profit. Therefore, it is strictly ordered that you should conduct a thorough enquiry in your *ilaqa* about this practice and send a report to the Government. If a detailed report regarding this matter is not received by the Government from you, and if in future you say that you do not know about it, your excuse shall not be heard. From an external source, it is learnt that one Government employee whosoever concerned to you has given room for proof, and you were to conduct enquiry into what he has done. Whatever profit he has made by such a practice may be thoroughly investigated and he must be punished accordingly. Why is it that the Government *ilaqadar*s are purchasing the grain at cheaper rates from the ryots and reselling it at higher rates in the capital and other *taluq*s, especially when there is a dearth of grain? The Government disapproves of this practice. It is to be enquired of them, the reason for the high price of grain and what they would suggest in order to overcome this. A report of the same must be submitted to the Government. You must also make every effort to stop the rise of prices in your *ilaqa* so that the ryots may be relieved of this dearth. The Government will be pleased by this. And if you suspect that some ryots or grain merchants in the *taluq*s are taking advantage of their well-to-do position, or the negligence of the tehsil revenue collectors, to hoard the grain and control the prices, which is troublesome for the common people, you must take suitable action for the common good of your people. You may kindly give your opinion in this regard and enforce it in your *taluq*s, but a report of it must be sent immediately to the Government. You must find out how much grain each person has in your *ilaqa* and the rate at which he has sold it. A statement of this kind must be prepared every week with details of the hire charges for transporting it to the capital. This may be mentioned either in Khandis or in Rollas. As soon as you gather this information, please send it. In addition, if during the search in your *ilaqa*, any grain from past years is found, it may be recovered and the Government informed of its quantity and quality. If it is possible by any means to send it to the capital, reasonable rates may be paid to the owners and obtained from the Government. The hire and other charges may be included and deducted by you. Any person who has stored the grain and not sold it is liable to be fined. You must treat this matter as most important and give it top priority. After receiving this order, you must complete your enquiry within four or five days and send a reply at the earliest.

ꙮ

No. 158
1859–60

Respected Sir

Pratab Som Pandit has delivered the letter and he has also spoken to me. According to the request of the bearer for caution and protection of the village, one horseman and two slaves may be posted. He may proceed carefully and cautiously.

ꕤ

No. 159
1859–60

Gracious Raja Sahib

The villages Do Jhar, etc., have been handed to Seshgir Rao. Hence, in this regard, the *zamindar*s of *pargana* Makhtal in every matter are harassing the ryots of the above-said village. It is certain that in the case of the above-cited village, you are helping the *zamindar*s of the village, and now you must not help them in any way.

[Signed] R. Inderjeeth Bil

ꕤ

No. 160
1859–60

Gracious Raja Sahib

One Arab *jawan* employee was sent along with a *mutasaddi* from *taluq* Koilkonda to carry Rs 500 H.S. [Halli Sicca]. Both of them spent the night at Farooqnagar. In the morning when the clerk got up, he saw that the Arab Jawan had absconded with the amount. The clerk has informed the *ilaqadar*s around Farooqnagar, which is the *ilaqa* of the Raja Sahib. Hence, it is requested that the Raja Sahib may help in arresting the above-said *jawan*. A poster may be pasted about this incident in Wanaparthy for his arrest. After arresting him, information may be sent to the *jamedar*. The physical description of the *jawan* is as follows: age, 50 years; height, average; colour, wheatish.

1860

No. 161
17 February 1860

Application:

Prior to this, I had submitted some applications to you that an amount of Rs 7,000 is due towards Raja Rameshwar Rao Bahadur of Wanaparthy. You have replied that you would settle the case. From that time onwards, I am waiting for your justice, but till now you have not decided the case even though the Raja Sahib came here, and it is heard that he has left very recently. Therefore, it is prayed that you may do justice with this already burdened person. It is submitted for your kindness.

Applicant: Abdul Karim, *saudagar*, Secunderabad

ଈ

No. 162
13 April 1860

Application of Allah Rakha, *saudagar*, addressed to Captain Fraser.

Raja Rameshwar Rao, Raja of Wanaparthy, bought two horses of Captain Metcalf Bahadur in an open auction on 15 February for Rs 800 and Rs 605 H.S. and paid Rs 400 Sugur Sicca. Kind Sir, in auction advertisement I have stated that these animals would be mortgaged to me until the full amount is paid. But, the Raja Sahib without paying me the full amount for both the animals has sold them. This is an injustice done to me. Hence, I have informed this to Captain [illegible] Bahadur who is the purchaser of the above-mentioned horses. The aforesaid Captain was requested to withhold the amount due till the matter is decided. But the aforesaid without waiting had paid the full amount to the Raja Sahib. Hence, I request an investigation may kindly be made in this case and justice done to me. I shall pray for you.

ଈ

No. 163
20 July 1860

From the Office of the Majlis.
For the information of Sawai Raja Rameshwar Rao Balwant Bahiri Bahadur.

An official letter dated 19 July 1860 and an application from the people, with a list of the seven thieves who were arrested along with their arms, have been received. In this regard, a petition for Rs 46 and 4 *annas* has also been received, as expenses incurred for the thieves. Therefore, it is ordered that this amount be noted in your accounts. From the statement given by the thieves, it has come to our knowledge that of the total number of weapons, four have been changed. Hence, you are ordered to send a report in this regard.

Kamdars exchanged at Narkonda: two. A long knife, a dagger.
Exchanged at Makhtal: two. An Abbasi sword, one other sword.

Receipt for Rs 46-4-0 from the Majlis.

ꟷ

No. 164
30 July 1860

From the Office of the Majlis.
For the information of Sawai Raja Rameshwar Rao Balwant Bahiri Bahadur.

A Government order, dated 4th of this month, in respect to deducting an amount of Rs 50 from the salary of the horseman Khaja Abdullah and disbursing it for the subsistence of his dependants, is enclosed herewith. This money may be given to Khaja Imamuddin, posted at Sugur, who may disburse the amount for the year 1852–53 along with the arrears for the year 1851–52 to the dependants of the aforesaid, according to the Government memo.

No. 165
17 August 1860

Seal: rectangular
Munsir Jung Bahadur

Gracious Raja Sahib

After eagerness to see you and wishing you happiness, this is to state that your letter dated the 15th of this month in reply to a letter written in Telugu in the case of Mallaiah Sahu, resident of Janumpet, and Smt. Teli Papiga and Vemangandla Luliah, etc., in which Pullaiah has agreed to pay four *tolas*. One *masha* gold and three missing *tolas* of gold, which were owed to him and to be paid, have been received. For the above, it may be acknowledged. At present, the impoverishment of Teli Papiga and the confessed statement of Pullaiah were written previously. Both the above-mentioned cases are pending for ten to twelve years. Those are to be submitted in the court to get them decided. The previous magistrate has left the office by transfer and the other is about to come. After his taking charge of the post, this case may be put up in the court, and whatever is decided, it may be acted upon accordingly and may be reported to you. Kindly let us know about your welfare by post.

ꟹ

No. 166
19 August 1860

From the Office of the Majlis.
For the information of Sawai Raja Rameshwar Rao Balwant Bahiri Bahadur.

A letter No. 1 on 20 July was in regard to your leave. The first condition is that on the 31st you must be here, but you have spent the whole month of Muharram away and you did not come. Hence, the Government states that it is against permission and has displeased the Government. Still, after this if you make delay, it would be most displeasing to the Government. Hence, it is to state that as soon as you receive this letter, you must depart from there and present yourself to the Government.

No. 167
21 August 1860

From the Office of the Majlis.
For the information of Sawai Raja Rameshwar Rao Balwant Bahiri Bahadur.

A copy of the letter from the police written in reply to the official letter from the Majlis, on the subject of Hasan and Sindhi, *jamedar*, is enclosed herewith. From it, it is evident that the constable took a horse and Rs 200 in cash from the dacoit Sukha Singh. The horse is still with the *jamedar* in your *ilaqa*. The Government has ordered that you be asked for a report regarding this case. Hence, it is stated that the required report must be sent to the Government immediately.

ꕥ

No. 168
2 September 1860

From the Office of the Majlis.
For the information of Sawai Raja Rameshwar Rao Balwant Bahiri Bahadur.

An order was issued on the 26th of last month to arrest Akbar Khan, an employee of the police, along with Jiya Rao. Now Muhammad Hussain, *mansabdar*, has submitted an application on a stamp paper in the Office of the Majlis, promising to pay a reward of Rs 200 to the person who captures him with the ornaments. Therefore, this letter is sent in continuation of the case.

ꕥ

No. 169
10 September 1860

Seal: rectangular
Mukhtar-ul-Mulk

Gracious Raja Sahib

It is learnt that thieves looted belongings worth Rs 400 from the house of Thota Sahebu, a farmer living in the hamlet Gadda, the village area of

Nandgaon, *jagir* of Raja-e-Rajayan Narayan Prashad Narender Bahadur, on 23 July of the present year. As you are the *maniwar* of that area, you are instructed to trace the thieves and arrest them with the stolen articles. These must be submitted to the Government and a receipt obtained. The thieves may be presented before the local criminal court for punishment.

ꕤ

No. 170
14 September 1860

Gracious Raja Sahib

It is learnt that Kalmi Cherla Laxmiah, a grain-merchant residing in Kesampeta, owes Rs. 200 to Mankot Ramiah, a grain-merchant of Bala Gunj bazaar. He gave the same of Kancha Kerla Laxmiah, another grain-merchant of the same bazaar as surety and promised to repay the money whenever it was demanded. However, now the aforesaid debtor is refusing to pay the amount. Therefore, it is written that he must be arrested and made to repay the money to Mankot Ramiah. The receipt for this may be sent here. If he again refuses to pay the amount due, he may be sent here so that his case may be submitted to the court.

ꕤ

No. 171
17 September 1860

From the Office of the Majlis.
For the information of Sawai Raja Rameshwar Rao Balwant Bahiri Bahadur.

A Government memo dated 29th of the last month in regard to your sending an urgent report of the particulars of Kukum Khan, Rohilla, prisoner, and the arrest of Nasrullah Khan in Gulbarga has been issued and is enclosed herewith. The required particulars may kindly be urgently sent here.

ꕤ

No. 172
22 September 1860

Gracious Raja Sahib

It is learnt that the Kotwal of Janumpet, Wanaparthy *taluq*, *pargana* Sugur, has forcibly brought away two bullocks from Allipur village, *patti* Palmoor belonging to the *jagir* of Durga Prasad. This action is disapproved of. Hence, it is ordered that the above-mentioned Kotwal must return the two bullocks of the *naib* of *patti* Palmoor, and a receipt of the same must be submitted to the Government.

ꟻↄ

No. 173
27 September 1860

From the Office of the Majlis.
For the information of Sawai Raja Rameshwar Rao Balwant Bahiri Bahadur.

In your letter dated 22 October 1860, you have requested that three *palas* gunpowder be sanctioned to you, as the gunpowder supplied to you earlier was spoiled when the storehouse collapsed. Accordingly, your request was submitted. However, it had been ordered that proper safety measures were to be adopted. As you did not follow instructions and were careless, you must submit the cost of the spoiled gunpowder to the Government, and no more gunpowder will be sanctioned to you.

ꟻↄ

No. 174
27 September 1860

From the Office of the Majlis.
For the information of Sawai Raja Rameshwar Rao Balwant Bahiri Bahadur.

On the 19th of the last month, a letter was written to send eighteen Government carts. Still the carts have not come. Those may be sent soon. Otherwise, send a reply by the staff bearer.

ജ

No. 175
29 September 1860

From the Office of the Majlis.
For the information of Sawai Raja Rameshwar Rao Balwant Bahiri Bahadur.

For enquiry in the cases of your *ilaqa* submitted to the Majlis, Tuesday is fixed. At the above-said day, you should come to the office of the Majlis in the afternoon. It is written by me in the presence of Muhammad Inayathullah.

ജ

No. 176
3 October 1860

From the Office of the Majlis.
For the information of Sawai Raja Rameshwar Rao Balwant Bahiri Bahadur.

Orders of the Government dated 1st of this month in regard to the information of any epidemic disease on the way to Bellary is to be given enclosed herewith. The information required to the Government may be sent immediately.

ജ

No. 177
3 October 1860

Seal: round
Revenue Board

From the Office of the Revenue Board.
For the information of Sawai Raja Rameshwar Rao Balwant Bahiri Bahadur.

Duvand Singh Sahu who lives in Makhtal cantonment has come to the Office of the Board to enquire about some cases. Hence, the aforesaid may be asked to be present in the Office of the Board with his account book of the year 1857–58.

ജ

No. 178
5 October 1860

From the Office of the Majlis.
For the information of Sawai Raja Rameshwar Rao Balwant Bahiri Bahadur.

In respect of your leave, it has been reported to the Government. It is ordered that at first a leave till 31 July was given to you and you have come after two months. At present, the said leave is not sanctioned.

ജ

No. 179
9 October 1860

From the Office of the Majlis.
For the information of Sawai Raja Rameshwar Rao Balwant Bahiri Bahadur.

On 7 October a letter (No. 26) issued from the office of the Majlis addressed to you by the opinion of the *ilaqadar*s of Nawab Shams-ul-Umra Bahadur was sent. A copy of the same is also now enclosed by which it shall be evident. As Syed Qutbuddin Hussain 2nd *ziladar* Sarikonda has written according to the order of the Government. Hence, it was ordered that although the above-cited letter written by the opinion of the *ilaqadar*s of the aforesaid Nawab was received by you, you have not acted on it. This letter is sent by *ghungru* mail.

ꕤ

No. 180
9 October 1860

From the Office of the Majlis.
For the information of Sawai Raja Rameshwar Rao Balwant Bahiri Bahadur.

On your leave application submitted to the Majlis, it is ordered that your leave is not sanctioned. Secondly, at present, in certain matters, you should report urgently. By this, the order first stated is statutory.

ꕤ

No. 181
10 October 1860

From the Office of the Majlis.
For the information of Sawai Raja Rameshwar Rao Balwant Bahiri Bahadur.

The documents in English have been submitted to the office of the Majlis by Haji Abdul Karim, a *saudagar* from Secunderabad, against you. One of them contains a claim of Rs 4,072-4-6, whereas in the second document, there is a claim of Rs 659-10-6 towards you. Another letter from the Resident has been received by the Government in this regard. The copies of both, the English letters as well as copies of the application from the aforesaid *saudagar*, are enclosed herewith. On the reverse of that application, in reply to the aforesaid Bahadur, signature was obtained stating that whatever amount by the opinion of Talib-ud-Daulah has been received, its entry has been taken in the Government account. Therefore, the procedure of payment is to prepare a separate bill for this. In such way, it is necessary for you that according to the Government memo, the amount of the *saudagar* may be paid and a reply may be sent immediately to the Majlis.

ꟈ

No. 182
11 October 1860

From the Office of the Majlis.
For the information of Sawai Raja Rameshwar Rao Balwant Bahiri Bahadur.

On the 11th of the past month and the 1st of the present month, in regard to the payment of the salary of Rajab Ali, resident of Bhurampet, and the salary of his horse is written. Till now you have not sent any report. The Government is pressing hard for this.

ꟈ

No. 183
October 1860

From the Office of the Majlis.
For the information of Sawai Raja Rameshwar Rao Balwant Bahiri Bahadur.

A copy of the application of Rajab Ali, signed by the Honourable Resident, received to the Majlis through the Government is enclosed herewith. The applicant has written about the horse and the salary of his horse. Your reply in this regard may be sent soon to be submitted in the Government.

ꟈ

No. 184
19 October 1860

Gracious Raja Sahib

From the application of Munsar Jung Bahadur, it is evident that Sri Rajiah, a goldsmith from Godal, who at present is staying in your *ilaqa*, is required for the investigation into the case of the ornaments and belongings that have been robbed. Despite letters from the above Bahadur, you have not sent the aforementioned goldsmith. Therefore, it is ordered that as soon as you receive this letter, you must send the aforesaid to the above-mentioned *taluqdar*. This is a Government memo.

༻

No. 185
24 October 1860

Gracious Raja Sahib

Mr. Sanders is travelling from the capital to Kurnool with his family and belongings. Therefore, wherever he halts on the way, you must supply him with the provisions required, and appoint someone to escort him safely and peacefully through your territory. Thereafter, you must submit a detailed report to the Government. No complaint of any kind should reach Government in this regard.

༻

No. 186
31 October 1860

For the information of Sawai Raja Rameshwar Rao Balwant Bahiri Bahadur.

An order from the Government, asking you to search for the plunderers of the halting place in Kesampalli, is sent herewith. In future, you must be careful regarding the maintenance of law and order in your territory, so that the Government check posts are not looted or damaged. You must make arrangements accordingly.

ꟷ

No. 187
1 November 1860

From the Office of the Majlis.
For the information of Sawai Raja Rameshwar Rao Balwant Bahiri Bahadur.

On the 10th of the last month, copies of the papers of the case of Haji Abdul Karim, *saudagar*, Secunderabad, were sent. Till now the reply regarding the above-mentioned is not received. The Majlis has told you in person that you had not sent the reply to these papers. The *naib* also has confessed and agreed to send the reply to the above case immediately, without any delay.

No. 188
6 November 1860

From the Office of the Majlis.
For the information of Sawai Raja Rameshwar Rao Balwant Bahiri Bahadur.

The Government has issued a memo today, enquiring about any epidemics prevalent in the area between Madhavaram, Makhtal and Secunderabad, and has instructed that a report to be sent urgently. Therefore, the necessary information must be sent immediately, as per the memo.

No. 189
15 November 1860

From the Office of the Majlis.
For the information of Sawai Raja Rameshwar Rao Balwant Bahiri Bahadur.

The Government memo issued at the end of the last month, ordering you to pay immediately an amount of Rs 2,645 to Tricher sahib as the first instalment as it has been fixed, is enclosed herewith. After its compliance, a reply may be given.

ဢ

No. 190
19 November 1860

Gracious Raja Sahib

From the application of Munsir Jung Bahadur, Government *taluqdar*, it is evident that the people of village Navcherla, *pargana* Sugur, of your *ilaqa* have obstructed the perennial stream, an irrigational source of village Madaipally, *pargana* Haveli Pangal, which from ancient times has run along the frontiers of village Navcherla. The ryots of Madaipally are cutting the trees that are at their boundary line to retain the water over which the people of Navcharla have their claim. They have started to level the boundary line to let the water of the stream spread in the jungle. At the time of this application of the aforesaid Bahadur without understanding it, you have instigated your *ilaqadar*s for riot. Moreover, the people of Rai Makal village in your *ilaqa* have carried away the earned goods of village Tigalpalli Pangal. These activities are disliked and are improper. Now you must bind your *ilaqadar*s not to break the above-cited stream, which is used for irrigation of village Madaipally, *pargana* Haveli Pangal. About the trees, the *panchayat* of the villages must decide it. Till it is decided, the above-said Bahadur, who oversees the disputed land, may lend it to the liquor sellers of other villages. The revenue thus obtained may be kept in his office, and after it is decided, it may be released to the party to whom it belongs. The earned goods of village Tigalpalli may be returned to them. The *panchayat* must decide about the disputed land of both the villages. No complaint of this kind may again come to this office. It is a strict Government memo.

ꕤ

No. 191
5 December 1860

From the Office of the Majlis.
For the information of Sawai Raja Rameshwar Rao Balwant Bahiri Bahadur.

Mirza Hussain Beg Naib Muhasib, Paigah *pargana* Chittapur, has kept nine Asamis of village Raenpalli, *ilaqa zamindar* Kakalvar, near him. You must take them from the aforesaid *naib* and give the receipt for this. Four Asamis of *ilaqa* Paigah who are in the village may be given back to the aforesaid *naib* and a receipt for this obtained. In future, any order issued in regard to the Asamis must be complied with.

ꕤ

No. 192
16 December 1860

Seal: rectangular
Munsir Jung Bahadur

Gracious Raja Sahib

Your letter of 8 December 1860 has been received in which you have informed us about the dismissal of eight cannoneers from the *ilaqa* of Commandant Muhammad Lal Mirza and claimed their salaries till the end of May–June of the present year, and stated to the Commandant that the aforesaid cannoneers' debt is received and he has known the facts. According to your request, we have written to Commandant Muhammd Lal Mirza in this regard and sent a report to the Government. Hence, it has been ordered in this regard that it may be acted on accordingly, and to be informed to you, without the orders of the Government, you may not make haste and do things in anticipation in such cases.

ꕤ

No. 193
31 December 1860

Benevolent Dear Friend Khan Sahib

Expressing my gratitude and conveying my hearty compliments, I have to state that a Banjara made his abode in village Amkunda, which is your *jagir*. He took a loan from Basappa Baqqal and absconded. After that he appeared before the *panchayat* and got it decided. It was learnt by a letter that the year before last, he caught four cows and either slaughtered them or changed their physical features. Dear friend, I do not know where Sokappa and Basappa Baqqal are living: nothing is heard about them or in what condition the grain merchant is in. Hence, it is to state for whom I should arrest so that a search for them may be made. At the receipt of this, you may kindly inform me about your welfare.

[Signed in English] Rameshwar

ഇ

No. 194
1860

Gracious Raja Sahib

The letters and papers of inspection from the postmaster of Hyderabad and the deputy postmaster of Makhtal and Musapet that were sent along with the letter of the Honourable Resident Bahadur have been received. It is learnt that on 19 October 1860, some armed dacoits attacked the Kesampalli check post at midnight. They injured the messengers, the constable and other constables of the Government post. They snatched their arms, took away their belongings and pulled down the check post. Some of the people went in search of these dacoits up to the village of Dhanwada in the *taluq* of Narayanpet, after which they lost track of the dacoits. Although they could not arrest the dacoits, these people thought that their search up to this place would absolve them of the blame. However, this was not approved of by the Government, and their efforts were not considered adequate to absolve them of their guilt. Therefore, it is ordered that the responsible people of Kesampalli who may have witnessed the incident or may have some information about it must take this matter seriously and help arrest the dacoits soon. In the future, they must take all precautions for safety and maintenance of law and order so that the people do not suffer any loss or injury again and the mail is not disrupted. You must consider this a warning. This is a Government memo.

ജ

No. 195
1860

Sir George Todd [illegible], Major No. 1633, aged 25 years, 2 months. Height 5 feet 8 ½ inches, colour reddish, eyes brown, newly appointed on 5 February 1853. Resident of London, profession blacksmith, red shirt, pajama grayish with a lot of self dress material. Absconding from 9 April 1860 from Bangalore.

ജ

No. 196
1860

Seal: rectangular
Mukhtar-ul-Mulk

Gracious Raja Sahib

Your petition dated 13 April 1860 has been received, in reply to the Government memo ordering you to pay Rs 1,000 as compensation to the *hundikar*, Muhammad Ali, a resident of Bombay. From this, it is learnt that the money has been given to Shah Yar-ul-Mulk. You must take this amount back from the aforesaid and credit it to the Government treasury. The matters for which you have requested information have been referred to Mutahawar Jung, who has been asked to report on them.

ജ

No. 197
1860

Gracious Raja Sahib

Your petition dated 16 June 1860 has been received, along with a chit and Rs 997 as part compensation for the articles stolen from Muhammad Ali, *hundikar*. A letter from Shah Yar-ul-Mulk, addressed to you, has also been received. The money has been disbursed to the *hundikar* with the consent of the Honourable Resident Bahadur. He has submitted another application along with a recommendation from the Honourable Resident Bahadur for the remaining amount that was looted, that is, Rs 1,656. In this regard, it is stated that as earlier two thieves from the *ilaqa* of *zamindar* Sangam, who were in collaboration with the thieves who looked like the *hundikar*, had been caught and that *zamindar* was held responsible for the theft. You had taken the responsibility of submitting the compensation on behalf of the *zamindar*, Sangam, and of arresting the thieves and producing them before the Government. No excuses will be entertained with regard to either the payment of the compensation to the *hundikar* or the presentation of the thieves before the Government. The letter from the Honourable Resident may be kindly returned.

1861

No. 198
8 January 1861

From the Office of the Majlis.
For the information of Sawai Raja Rameshwar Rao Balwant Bahiri Bahadur.

A letter No. 198 dated 28 December 1860 in English along with a petition and letter of the *jawans* is received and the matter of the three papers was submitted to the Government. It was ordered that for the sake of *inam*, the Government does not terminate the services of the people. Moreover, there is no vacancy in other platoons.

No. 199
13 January 1861

Abdullah bin Ali

Order in the name of Rani Ankai, wife of Subba Reddi, *deshmukh* of *patti* Rachala, *pargana* Kandur, *sarkar* Ghanapur, *subah* Farkhunda Bunyad, Hyderabad. In accordance with her petition and based on the agreement submitted to the Government, this order is being given, granting the aforesaid *patti* Rachala in the *pargana* mentioned above, under the head of lease [*tahud*] for a period of three years from the beginning of the year 1859–60 till the end of 1861–62 for an amount of Rs 55,878 in regard to goods, remaining revenue, liquor tax, village artisan tax, garden, irrigated land, tree tax, *rusum* and the tax on mango trees. Now she must be satisfied, and see that the old and new ryots are kept happy and content. She must try to increase their numbers and improve cultivation. According to the agreement, the amount to be paid to the Government should be submitted regularly every year after the harvest. Receipts must be obtained for the same. This is a permanent order and should be acted upon.

ᘓ

No. 200
10 February 1861

From the Office of the Majlis.
For the information of Sawai Raja Rameshwar Rao Balwant Bahiri Bahadur.

In reply to the suit of Haji Abdul Karim, *saudagar*, Secunderabad, it is again and again being written to you to report whether the amount of the suit above-said is received in consultation with the late Talib-ud-Daulah. An attested copy of the case was sent to you and in that it was written that the above amount may be adjusted in the Government accounts. Hence, the first condition is separate. For this, what you have reported is a reply to the previous letter.

According to your report and according to the petitions of the *saudagar*, it has been reported to the Government. Thus, it is ordered that a detailed report may be collected that Talib-ud-Daulah has demanded that amount. Hence, it is to state that you may report whether you have received it. The details may be written to be reported to the Government.

ꙮ

No. 201
18 February 1861

From the Office of the Majlis.
For the information of Sawai Raja Rameshwar Rao Balwant Bahiri Bahadur.

A letter in English No. 6 dated 12 January 1861 along with seven cannoneers (terminated) have come to the Majlis and they were presented before the Government.

ꙮ

No. 202
2 March 1861

From the Office of the Majlis.
For the information of Sawai Raja Rameshwar Rao Balwant Bahiri Bahadur.

A letter No. 34 dated 10th of the last month was sent with instructions to send a report about the amount to be received from late Talib-ud-Daulah because it is required in the suit filed by Haji Abdul Karim, but no reply has been received from you till now. A long period has passed. The copy of the businessman's application is also sent herewith, and request you to give a reply in regard to letter No. 34 as required by the Government.

ꙮ

No. 203
7 March 1861

From the Office of the Majlis.
For the information of Sawai Raja Rameshwar Rao Balwant Bahiri Bahadur.

A Government memo was sent to you today with orders to have a search conducted for the bullock that was lost by a head constable at Bala Palli. Further orders that are enclosed herewith state that the above-mentioned bullock should be sent to the Government. You must comply with these orders.

ꣻ

No. 204
20 April 1861

Copy of orders under the seal of Nawab Mukhtar-ul-Mulk Bahadur

To Munsir Jung Bahadur

Dear Sir

It is evident that an amount of Rs 2,000 of customary district revenue in substitute to the plunder of the village Telkapalle in the jurisdiction of Kishan Rao *taluqdar* (suspended), which was confiscated by the Government, is due. In spite of search by intelligence officers of *ilaqa* Gopalpet and the people who had submitted it, the amount is still not with the Government. Therefore, this is to state that if the above-cited amount plundered of the above-mentioned village has been handed over to the Government by the *ilaqadar*s of Gopalpet, it is to be paid to the agent of Raja Rameshwar Rao Balwant Bahiri Bahadur. The customary district revenue belonging to your *taluq* may be continued to be paid to him in accordance with the established procedure.

ꣻ

No. 205
24 April 1861

Seal: rectangular
Mukhtar-ul-Mulk

Gracious Raja Sahib

Taxes on salt from Machlibandar are to be consigned to Muhammad Abdus Salam, the officer at the *taluq*, under the head of revenue. The services of Kanda Swami have been terminated by the Government with effect from 13 March 1861. The merchants and businessmen who bring salt from the *ghat*s of Kala Chabutra to Sugur and the *taluq* of Makhtal for sale may apply the tax as usual to the *chaukidar*s of Makhtal for sale and may pay the tax as usual to the *taluq* officer of Achampet. In cases pertaining to the above-mentioned *taluq*, you may help the aforesaid *chaukidar*s in this matter. This is a strict Government memo.

ઇ

No. 206
10 May 1861

Copy of the orders under the seal of Nawab Mukhtar-ul-Mulk Bahadur.

To Safi-ud-Daula Bahadur

It is learnt that you have stopped the payment of customary district revenue to the *naib* of Raja Rameshwar Rao Balwant Bahiri Bahadur for his *ilaqa* villages Avancha and Kalwakurthy because he has not carried out his duties in a befitting manner in this post. Therefore, this is to state that the requisite rights, *rusum* and *abwab* pertaining to the above-said post may be released to the agent of the aforesaid Raja Sahib so that he may continue with the administration of the post.

ઇ

No. 207
10 May 1861

Copy of the orders under the seal of Nawab Mukhtar-ul-Mulk Bahadur

To Sultan Nawaz-ul-Mulk Bahadur

Dear Raja Sahib

The file for the release of the customary revenue of the villages of Yeljal and Korangal belonging to Raja Rameshwar Rao Balwant Bahiri Bahadur and the nomination for the post of district revenue accountant is before me. This is to state that according to the established practice the right of fees and *abwab* of the district revenue accountant is to be paid to the agent of the aforesaid Raja. The person nominated may reply for the administration of the above-cited post.

ஐ

No. 208
11 May 1861

Seal: rectangular
Mutahawwar Jung

Gracious Happy Lad

You have sent a letter dated 3rd of the last month along with Captain Young and your younger brother requesting a loan of Rs 2,000 Sicca Company for your needs and informed me about its receipt. That was the end of the year, and the decision of the *tehsil* and the compensation under the head of paid in full was submitted to the ruler. The statement of fact by you astonished me much, but to keep your dignity and at your request I again gave Rs 1,000 Sicca Company to you and you executed the document in which you promised to repay it in two months. It is better you clear off the loan within the promised period because I have to submit it to the Government.

ஐ

No. 209
23 May 1861

For the information of Sawai Raja Rameshwar Rao Balwant Bahiri Bahadur.

Your letter No. 9 of this month has been received regarding the injuries to the sepoys of the halting place of the English post office. Reports from the headmen and accountants of village [illegibile] and Mandepally, in *taluq* Narayanpet, with regard to the above-cited incident have also been received. Therefore, it is ordered that compensation must be paid for the loss suffered by the *jawan*s of the post office.

ꕥ

No. 210
29 May 1861

From the Office of the Majlis.
For the information of Sawai Raja Rameshwar Rao Balwant Bahiri Bahadur.

In the case of the dismissed cannoneers, the details you have sent have been submitted to the Government. The memo for releasing their salaries has not yet been issued from the office. As soon as it is issued, it will be sent to you.

ꕥ

No. 211
29 May 1861

For the information of Sawai Raja Rameshwar Rao Balwant Bahiri Bahadur.

Your letter has been received which gave me information. According to the Government orders, the Risala of Deccani horsemen of Venkat Sahib Bahadur, etc., would decamp to Raichur on 1st July 1861, Monday.

Hence, the seamen and others may be bound to be present at the Kala Chabutra *ghat* and some *jawan*s may be posted to help them.

Appa Rao Naib, *pargana* Makhtal.

ဨ

No. 212
3 June 1861

Copy. For the information of Sawai Raja Rameshwar Rao Balwant Bahiri Bahadur, Head of the Makhtal cantonment.

Letter dated 29th of the present year stating that your Risala is posted under me and to keep it near my camp and on 1st of this month, at the time being, the syce and horsemen are to be sent to Raichur.

As these are the rainy days and without any halting place it is most difficult to get horsemen in Raichur, therefore, no cruelty may be done to the ryots. The syce and horses may be kept with the horsemen, and they may be bound strictly not to tease the ryots.

The horsemen may be strictly bound that they may pay the cost of the commodities that they buy from the villages according to the rate fixed and may not act against it.

The names of the High Officer and other officers such as head constable and deputy head constable who are among the horsemen may be informed by me.

The horsemen may be warned that they may cooperate with the agent of the people who are appointed by me and are staying at Raichur. And whatever order I shall issue, they must obey it.

At this place, it is the custom of the English people to pay one *anna* per allotment for the bullocks of the carts and one *paisa* to the begar. This custom may be followed by the horsemen, and they must not act against it and may not press the ryots.

This day, it is 3rd of the present month; the letter of the syce is received and it is replied.

No. 213
12 June 1861

From the Office of the Majlis.
For the information of Sawai Raja Rameshwar Rao Balwant Bahiri Bahadur.

An order addressed to you was issued today, instructing you to be ready with your cavalry. Thus, it was ordered; but since protection for your ladies is also necessary, you may stay there for the time being. You must be ready to leave as soon as you receive the second order, but until the second order reaches you, you must not leave your territory.

ꝏ

No. 214
16 June 1861

From the Office of the Majlis.
For the information of Sawai Raja Rameshwar Rao Balwant Bahiri Bahadur.

The Government memo addressed to Munsir Jung Bahadur in the case of payment of salaries to the canon firers is enclosed and sent to him. You may act accordingly.

ꝏ

No. 215
23 June 1861

Gracious Raja Sahib

Your letter of 19th of this month along with the Government memo has been received. A receipt for an amount of Rs 472 towards the salaries of eight cannoneers from the *ilaqa* of Muhammad Lal Mirza Commandant with effect from 17 August 1860 till 10 July 1861 has also been received. As the cultivation for this year is not good, out of the amount mentioned in the receipt, an amount of Rs 200 in cash is sent with the bearers of this letter, Shaikh Imam and Syed Imam. The remaining Rs 272 may be collected by sending your horsemen at the end of this month.

ꙮ

No. 216
23 June 1861

From the Office of the Majlis.
For the information of Sawai Raja Rameshwar Rao Balwant Bahiri Bahadur.

Enclosed herewith are the orders from the Government, along with a copy of the document from Dar-ul-Adalat, regarding the case of Venkat Narsu, the alleged murderer of Maulvi Sibghatullah. From these, it is evident that the alleged murderer was required by the court of law, but according to the order from the criminal court, he has been released.

ꙮ

No. 217
27 June 1861

From the Office of the Majlis.
For the information of Sawai Raja Rameshwar Rao Balwant Bahiri Bahadur.

This is a Government memo instructing you to proceed to Raichur with all your cannons and other equipment, and to perform the Government duties according to the advice of Mir Mumin Ali, *taluqdar*.

ꙮ

No. 218
28 June 1861

From the Office of the Majlis.
For the information of Sawai Raja Rameshwar Rao Balwant Bahiri Bahadur.

From the report of Venkat Rao, a Government clerk, it is learnt that Nandnoor Venkaiah, *ilaqadar* of the above-said clerk, is residing at present in Narolavelly village, *pargana* Yeljal, for his medical treatment. The wife of the aforesaid *ilaqadar* went to bring water from the well on the 23rd of the current month. Seeing the woman alone, thieves caught hold of her and snatched away her ornaments, as detailed in the list enclosed herewith. As the post of district revenue accountant of the above-mentioned village has been assigned to you, you must, therefore, bind your agent of the place. This theft is astonishing because it occurred in broad daylight and in the midst of that locality. Conduct an investigation into this theft so that the thieves may quickly be arrested, and the goods recovered and returned to the owner. The criminals must be punished accordingly. In this regard, a strict warning must be written to your agent; otherwise you will be required to give your explanation for this.

No. 219
1861

Compensation for the ornaments looted and stolen at village Tardavelli, *pargana* Yeljal, *jagir* Abdullah Khan Mandozi, from Sandival Venkiah, *ilaqa* Venkat Rao, Government clerk on 23 June 1861.

Karsa: one pair, 20 *tolas*.
Bangle: one, 6 *tolas*.
Gold: 35 *tolas*, 8 *mashas*.
Finger rings: one, 5 *tolas*, 8 *mashas*.
Hakku: one, 7 *tolas*.

No. 220
1861

Seal: rectangular
Mukhtar-ul-Mulk

Gracious Raja Sahib

Your petition dated 5 March 1861 and that of Venkat Narsu, the plunderer who allegedly robbed the belongings of Maulvi Sibghatullah, have both been received. The above-mentioned robber was produced before the criminal court of the capital. A *fatwa* has been received by the Government, a copy of which is enclosed herewith for your information. From the same, it is evident that the aforesaid person is not guilty. Hence, he has been released. This is for your information.

No. 221
1861

Gracious Rani Sahiba

Colonel Commander Sahib Bahadur of the Government Artillery left Secunderabad and reached Shamshabad on 23 January 1861 of the current year and from there has proceeded to Kurnool. Therefore, while his regiment is in your estate, two pairs of bullocks on hire charges may be provided to them so that no complaint reaches the Government in the regard. The hire charges may not be claimed from him but from the Government; after you receive this advice, the formal claim may be put to the Government. This is a Government memo.

No. 222
3 June 1863

Petition submitted to the great ruler.

Narsa Bai, wife of Venkat Krishna Reddi, *deshmukh* of the *patti* of Rachala, *pargana* of Kandur, stated that all the shareholders had unanimously decided to adopt one boy in the year 1856–57. In the same way, they are adopting a boy of their choice this time too. We would like the boy to flourish and lead a comfortable life. Since you are the highest authority, we request you to grant us permission to adopt the boy.

We are your humble servants.

1864–1868

No. 223
25 January 1868

Translation of a letter of Deputy Assistant Quarter Master General Mysore Division addressed to the Honourable Resident Bahadur dated 25 January 1868.

We have been informed that the 10th Regiment in which ten English officers, 419 soldiers, sixty-three ladies, 126 children, 1,200 labourers and common people, 600 bullocks, twenty horses, ten elephants and 88 camels are coming from the north of the Dominion. According to the way mentioned, the rein would halt at different places. On the 3rd this month 1868, they would come to Kyatur.

Your grace according to the list sent by the Commandant of the Regiment to you, you may kindly give orders for the supply of provision. In case there is any epidemic in the way of which you had not sent any information here, you may kindly send it to the aforesaid under intimation of this office.

3 March Kyatur
4 March Bikkam
5 March Venkatapur
6 March Mallepalle
7–8 March Kothakota
9 March Atkal
10 March Janumpet
11 March Poddatur
12 March Jadcherla
13 March Balanagar or Nakampally
14–15 March Farooqnagar

16 March Palmakole
17 March Shamshabad
18 March Dargah, Barhane Shah
19 March Secunderabad

You may also order them to keep clean the above-mentioned halting places, and the amount of their expenses may be drawn by a contingency bill from this office.

Rice 516 lbs.
Grass 2193 lbs.
Gram 588 lbs.
Milk 25 cans
Eggs 9 [illegible]
Labour 20

ᘓ

No. 224
9 October 1868

A report from the Honourable Resident Bahadur has brought to our notice that at three places in Wanaparthy District, the Government road has been flooded over and has sunk for long distances. There are also no electric poles. This means that the owners of those holdings have stored too much water and thus caused inconvenience to travellers. The travellers now have to make a detour of one or two miles and undergo several difficulties. You must see that such hindrances do not recur at the mentioned places. A report regarding this matter may be sent at once. It is very urgent.

Secondly, such hindrances must not occur on this highway, as it is the only route connecting Hyderabad and Calcutta. Therefore, the Rani Sahiba is requested to pay attention to these Government orders and see that arrangements are made to lower the water level up to the foot of the electric poles. Otherwise, it will be understood that she does not intend to allow the road to be used for Government purpose.

ᘓ

No. 225
4 December 1868

Seal
Mukhtar-ul-Mulk

Gracious Raja Sahib

The salt tax of Machlibandar for the *ilaqa* officer has been consigned as revenue to Bapuji by the Government. From your letter, it is evident that the receipt of compensation was based on management. An outpost at *ghat* Yaparla is necessary. Therefore, this is to state that the officers and *ilaqadar*s may establish their own outposts at the *ghat*. You may not prevent them doing so, and, in fact, you may help them in every case pertaining to the *taluq* officers.

ꙮ

No. 226
1868–69

Gracious Raja Sahib

From the report and map sent by the Honourable Resident Bahadur with regard to the road between Bellary and Kurnool, your discourse with Mr. Mart in your estate has come to our notice. It is clear that you have opposed him. Therefore, this is written to remind you that the road is a public one and all the people may use it. You must not impose unnecessary impediments. At the time of construction on your land, the Government must not receive any complaints.

ꙮ

No. 227
1868–69

Gracious Raja Sahib

Your letter has been received. According to your request, orders in the name of Ghulam Qadir, the Qadi of Jatprole, have been issued and referred to Hasanuddin Khan, depending on the judgment given in the case of the murder of Jan Muhammad Khan Billouch. The case is being tried according to Muslim law.

ꕤ

No. 228
1868–69

Seal
Mukhtar-ul-Mulk

Gracious Raja Sahib

From a letter of the Honourable Resident Bahadur, it is learnt that the mischief-maker Bhim Rao has fled from the Nizam's territory along with some of his confederates towards the southern part of Maratha territory and has taken refuge in the Kuppal fort. It is therefore ordered that you must strictly warn your people in Sugur and your other *ilaqas* to keep watch at the boundaries of your estate to see that the aforesaid and his associates do not enter Government territory. If they do, they must be immediately arrested and imprisoned.

ꕤ

No. 229
1868–69

Detailed list of articles supplied to 'E' Company.

Goats 4
Hens 30
Chickens 10
Flour meal 50 *seers*
Dal 25 *seers*
Salt 13 *seers*
Coriander 5 *seers*
Pepper 5 *seers*
Onions 10 *seers*
Ghee 5 *seers*

Jaggery 16 *seers*
Tar 12 *seers*
Oil 12 *seers*
Jowar 16 *seers*
Hay 20 bundles
Gram 50 *seers*
Turmeric 12 *seers*
Fuel 200 *seers*

ᢒ

No. 230
1868–69

Seal
Mansoor-ud-Daulah

Aziz-ul-Qadr Rani Sahiba

My sons Syed Fateh Ali Khan and Syed Ibrahim Ali Khan are going to Hyderabad along with their dependants. You may provide an armed escort to accompany them up to the boundaries of your territory. With best compliments.

ᢒ

No. 231
1868–69

Gracious Raja Sahib

An advertisement written in Telugu with a duplicate and a stamp of 14 *annas* and 6 paisa sent by the Civil Judge, Nandyal, enclosed with a letter of the Resident Bahadur have been received. It is ordered that on the reverse of the said advertisement, the signature of Mahjan Majas, resident of Wanaparthy, may be affixed and returned within a fortnight to the Government, and the duplicate may be given to the aforesaid.

ᢒ

No. 232
1868–69

Gracious Raja Sahib

An advertisement written in Telugu with respect to the arresting of the prisoners who had escaped from the Machlibandar prison and the letter of the Resident Bahadur enclosed with it are received. Therefore, it is ordered that the advertisement may be posted in your territory at public places.

ဆ

No. 233
1868–69

Seal
Mukhtar-ul-Mulk

Gracious Raja Sahib

In your *ilaqa*, the Government clerks are still collecting road taxes in some villages of this Government. Therefore, it is now stated clearly that you must watch over your *ilaqa* and administer it well. The *naib*s, *zamindar*s and contractors, etc., under your *ilaqa* may be strictly ordered to honour the agreement of business that has been signed between the two Governments. By this agreement, the collection of the road tax from the merchants of this State who are transporting goods from the merchants of this State has been abolished. Accordingly, you must make arrangements in all your *ilaqa*s, so that the merchants transporting goods from one part of the State to another do not have to pay road taxes in any of the Government territories, including yours. If any *ilaqadar* goes against this order, and collects the road tax, he will be severely punished. No reasons or excuses will be entertained. However, every merchant who transports goods from one place to another within the State has to pay 5 per cent of the selling price wherever he sells his goods. If he purchases goods within the State, to sell outside, a 5 per cent tax may be levied on the cost price of the article.

ဆ

No. 234
1868–69

Gracious Raja Sahib

A notice regarding the exemption of road tax on grain that is transported to the capital and the cantonments of Chadderghat, Secunderabad and Alwal is enclosed herewith. Though the road tax on permits is exempted by the Government, again it is to state that in your *ilaqa*s, you may bind the merchants to get the permits from the Government and then to transport the grains to the capital and the above-mentioned cantonments. The road tax permit may not be collected by them for any reason whatsoever. In case revenue collectors or *chaukidar*s collect the road or other taxes, they will be severely punished by the Government.

ꙮ

No. 235
1868–69

Seal
Mukhtar-ul-Mulk

Gracious Raja Sahib

Captain Sahib Bahadur, Superintendent of Police, Secunderabad, has enquired about the nature of the crops cultivated during the present year. Therefore, it is stated that a detailed report of the crops cultivated during this year may be sent to the Government.

ꙮ

No. 236
1868–69

Seal
Mukhtar-ul-Mulk

Gracious Raja Sahib

The Commissioner General of Secunderabad has enquired about the nature of the crops cultivated during the present year. Therefore, it is stated that a detailed report of the crops cultivated during this year may be sent to the Government.

ꕥ

No. 237
1868–69

Seal

Gracious Raja Sahib

A Government memo addressed to you has been issued stating that the report of the summer crop of this year may be sent, giving details of the total grain produced and the quantity sent to the capital after deducting the requirements of the ryots in your *ilaqa*. After examining the report, Government orders will be issued, which should be complied with.

ꕥ

No. 238
1868–69

Gracious Raja Sahib

The Government has received a letter from the Resident Bahadur and one from the Chief Secretary to the Government of Madras. From these letters, it is evident that engineers are being sent to survey the land, for the purpose of constructing a road for the steam carriages from Kutti via Kurnool to Hyderabad. Therefore, this is to state that upon their arrival at Janumpet, Mumarelly, Kothakota, Mallepalle, Venkatapur and Makram, etc., which are in your *ilaqa*, you must supply them with adequate provisions and help them in every possible way. When they reach the boundaries of the Government, the *mansabdar*s will be sent. The provisions may be supplied as mentioned above.

ꕥ

No. 239
1868–69

Copy of the orders of Nawab Siraj ul Mulk Bahadur

Gracious Raja Sahib

By the ruler's court, the services of *tehsildar*, *pargana* Sugur and Kothakota, *sarkar* Pangal, *subah* Farkhunda Bunyad are taken away from Talib-ud-Daulah since the beginning of the year 1851–52 and in his place Muhammad Aminuddin of *ilaqa* Jan Baz Jung Bahadur is appointed. Hence, you must appear before him and pay the Government amount year-wise and crop-wise. You must not delay or show any hesitation in this regard.

ꟾ

No. 240
1868–69

Gracious Raja Sahib

Arrangements for the case of Ghulam Dastagir are well known. A Telugu paper of Antim Pandit is enclosed herewith, which would be received. As the elder people have orally said to grant two *anna*s daily allowance and two *anna*s annually, you may kindly honour me by a *sanad* of the same and get it to me when you would come to Balapur.

Request of application of Bala Prashad.

No. 241
1868–69

Seal
Mukhtar-ul-Mulk

Gracious Raja Sahib

Translation of the report sent by Colonel Taren Bahadur regarding the subject that healthy young trained bullocks would be kept ready to pull the cart of the aforesaid Bahadur to take him to Kurnool. This has given a shock to the Englishmen in your *ilaqa*. A copy of the translation of his letter is enclosed herewith stating why such a thing has happened and what is the cause for it; this in spite of your promise to supply the bullocks of the said condition in your *ilaqa*. Explanation of this incident is your responsibility. You must send a report immediately to satisfy the Government and the aforesaid Bahadur. According to the letter of Sheik Daud, Superintendent of Government, in the future, if you do not have good bullocks in your *ilaqa*, you must keep the young bullocks of good health and proper training which the Government desires. Your present attitude is totally disliked by the Government, that you are so negligent in Government matters. Either you are personally involved in it or the aforesaid Superintendent is also with you to disobey the Government orders and create hurdles to the smooth work of the Government.

ཱ

No. 242
1868–69

Seal

Mukhtar-ul-Mulk

Gracious Raja Sahib

Orders were issued regarding the maintenance of bullocks in the villages of your *ilaqa* for pulling the carriages of the Englishmen. However, a letter from Sheikh Daud who has been appointed by the Government to investigate and give a report of the accident that makes it evident that the *ilaqadar*s taking advantage of your absence have not yet made any arrangements for him. Therefore, this is to state that according to the previous orders, young healthy and trained bullocks chosen by Sheikh Daud may be allotted for his transport. You must send a report regarding this matter to the Government immediately.

No. 243
1868–69

Respected Courteous Raja Sahib

I, humble Abdul Qader, tailor, after paying homage and respect by kneeling down and saluting you, state that as per your order, I took six spindles and twelve red dyes from Gulab Khan and gave it to Raunaq Baksh. Raunaq Baksh took two *thans* at a cost of Rs 9 through Kale Khan, *jamedar*, and asked me to pay it. Further, the materials of red dyes, etc., have also been given. It is for your kind information. Moreover, he has demanded the spindles. Gulab Khan till now has taken one pair of textiles. One *than* and blouse, and a pair of bangles for Rani Sahiba are to be prepared because this pair is not suitable for you. You bless me always by your favours.

ꟿ

No. 244
1868–69

Dear Raja Sahib

Village Lumalpally, *pargana* Nar'khora, *sarkar* Muhammadnagar, *subah* Farkhunda Bunyad, Hyderabad, *jagir* of Hussain Munawwar Khan, is sanctioned as *zat jagir* to dervish Munawwar Khan, etc., sons of the aforesaid Khan with effect from 1815–16 according to the documents. Now you may approach them and cultivate their permission by paying fixed and proper revenue in time. It is a strict Government memo.

ꟿ

No. 245
1868–69

Seal
Mir Ezad Yar Khan
Servant of Asaf Jah Bahadur

High dignity Janaki *zamindarni pargana* Sugur

Your *vakil* Malam Bhat attended the court and was honoured. The other thing to state is that all the affairs may be corrected and at the receipt of this letter, according to your agreement and loyalty, you may hand over the village to the Government in lieu of the compensation and get the blessing of the ruler.

ঌ

No. 246
1868–69

Gracious Raja Sahib

Maintenance in all respect has been sanctioned from there only. For the same reason, your petition along with an amount of Rs 3,000 *nazrana* was submitted, and a *sanad* under the seal of Raja Sahib Raja Ram Kishan Bahadur with a title of Sawai Rai is enclosed herewith. Now, as soon as you see this letter, send Rs 1,000 towards the title, although you have agreed upon Rs 2,000 for the fixed *sanad*. Keeping in view to let you survive, I have requested that you may be allowed to pay Rs 1,000 more. But it was not agreed upon and with a hope that you shall send the above-mentioned amount, a *sanad*, ornamented shawl and a title was issued to you with great efforts. The *sanad* is so perfect in its matter that I have not seen it before. The matter is like this that you have submitted Rs 2,000, and Rs 1,000 are remaining at your side. I stood surety for the above-said amount and obtaining the above-mentioned article that I have sent them through your *vakil* Venkat Narsu. Now without wasting a single moment, you must submit the amount. No delay should be made. Remaining particulars could be known by your *vakil*.

ঌ

No. 247
1868–69

Gracious Raja Sahib

Eight months have passed and still you have not submitted Rs 12,000 to the Government under the head *peshkash* and *nazrana*. Hence, it is decided that you should submit it with interest. Further, it is to state that in future if you do not want to keep friendly terms and still want to retain the *samasthan*, no sooner than you receive this order, you must submit the above-cited amount, and in case you make further any delay, it would not be good for you.

ꕤ

No. 248
1868–69

Seal
Mukhtar-ul-Mulk

Gracious Raja Sahib

From the letter of the Resident Bahadur, it is learnt that the unemployed Rohillas, Arabs and other mischievous elements have gathered in the forests of Nirmal and Mahur. One troop belonging to General Sir Hewroses' army has been posted at Mallupet, which is on the Hyderabad route. This arrangement is necessary so that the miscreants in small troops from forests do not enter the capital Hyderabad. Therefore, this is to state that every mischievous Rohilla and Arab who is found on the road or in the forest of your *ilaqa* may be imprisoned immediately and sent to the capital. In case he is a Government employee and is not associated with the miscreants, a reliable person may be asked to stand surety for him after which he may not be harassed. If you are negligent in arresting the above-mentioned miscreants, you will be held responsible by the Government.

ꕤ

No. 249
1868–69

Seal
Mukhtar-ul-Mulk

Gracious Raja Sahib

Some *taluqdar*s have written that it is a long-standing tradition to submit the excess revenue amount of the villages, though it be of *jagir*, *inam* or fixed rate lands into the Government accounts of the *pargana* concerned. At present, with the permission of the ruler, the taxes on articles of villages of *jagir* are taken into the accounts of Government excess revenue. Therefore, this is to state that the taxes for the export of agricultural produce or industrial items from any place could be taken by the *ilaqadar* concerned. Therefore, whatever the productive articles and industries of the *jagir* may be, chits may be issued to the *jagirdar*s so that they can move their articles within the boundaries of the State without being stopped by any authority. You may not demand taxes on the export of productive articles and industrial items from the *jagirdar*s of your *ilaqa* for any reason.

ഌ

No. 250
1868–69

Gracious Raja Sahib

A summons written in Telugu with a duplicate of the same along with the letter of the Resident Bahadur and a stamp of 14 *anna*s are sent by the Judge of Kurnool. Therefore, it is ordered that on the reverse of the notice, the signature of Purkaliya, resident of Ramkishtapur, may be taken and returned to the Government and the duplicate may be given to him.

ഌ

No. 251
1868–69

Gracious Raja Sahib

A summons in Telugu with its copy, a letter from the Honourable Resident Bahadur and a stamp of 14 *anna*s and 6 *paisa* sent by the Judge, Kurnool, have been received. You are ordered to obtain the signature of Tarkalliya, son of Shiv Ramappa, a resident of Ramkishtapur, *pargana* Wanaparthy, on the reverse of the above-cited summons and return it to the Government within a fortnight. The copy may be given to the aforesaid.

No. 252
1868–69

Gracious Raja Sahib

After best compliments, it is to state that I have received your letter and felt happy to read it. The copy of the ruling is enclosed herewith, and as per your desire, I got a house vacated for you.

No. 253
1868–69

Gracious Raja Sahib

A petition in Telugu sent by the *takiddar* has been received, regarding the murder of a traveller, which was committed near Chauki Chashma. The murdered man's belongings have been found at Chauki Kothakota. A letter from the Honourable Resident Bahadur is enclosed herewith in this regard. Now, this is to state that as the district revenue accountant of the said place has been assigned to you, it is your responsibility to send a report about this immediately to the Government, so that the same may be conveyed to the Honourable Resident Bahadur.

No. 254
18 June 1869

In its decision to settle the accounts of the moneylenders of Mirza Muhammad Beg, the Government has stated that in spite of giving orders to the *zamindar* of Sugur to pay off the amount that he owes, he has not complied with the orders. Hence, a staff-holder of the Government has been sent to the *vakil* of the aforesaid *zamindar* in order to claim the amount at once and pay it off to the moneylenders of Mirza Muhammad Beg. If any delay is caused, then the staff-holder is advised to report it to the Government so that an order may be given to the chief *taluqdar* of the district to summon the respondent. Hence, it must be written immediately to Raja Sahib to claim the amount within ten days, and if it is not sanctioned, this information must be reported to the Government.

[Signed] Shanker Rao

༺༻

No. 255
2 August 1869

Seal
Mukhtar-ul-Mulk

Gracious Raja Sahib

Babu Gosayin Daheja Dhari, along with a gold sash, ten riding horses and forty people, is travelling from the capital to the Sri Balaji *jatra*. Therefore, you are ordered to provide two foot soldiers to accompany them while crossing the Krishna River so that they do not encounter any hindrances. This is an order and must be complied with.

༺༻

No. 256
4 September 1869

From the Secretary, Government Courts of Law, Hyderabad Dominion.

It has been brought to my notice that the *zamindar*s and ryots of a village near Sugur owe an amount to the late Habib bin Hamed al Hadari, resident of village Madri. Hence, this is to state that if the successors of the deceased filed a suit, you must make a thorough enquiry and arrange for the payment of the same and inform this department.

ꙮ

No. 257
6 September 1869

Respected Rani Sahiba

The application of late Raja Rameshwar Rao dated 30th of the last month was put before me, and by enquiry into the case, whatever Raja Sahib has submitted through Seshgir Rao Vakil caused agony. Nobody could do against the will of God. Therefore, without trying to seek anything, you must keep patience. Moreover, whatever considerations and favours were bestowed on Raja Sahib, more than that would be bestowed on you from the Government. Therefore, now you may be satisfied and take care of the dependants and your house. Whatever subsistence is given by the Government, it should be known to all the *ilaqadar*s, and they must not misunderstand it. In case anyone faces a natural death as the above-said Raja, it may be informed to the Government. The late aforesaid Raja in case of adoption had submitted an application. From his relatives, whosoever has more right, he may be adopted and sanction may be taken by writing to the Government.

ꙮ

No. 258
9 September 1869

Prior to this, on 20th of the last month, papers of account were submitted by Haji Zakariya Khan seeking a reply in return. However, till now, you have not given a reply. Hence, this is written to inform you that you must submit your reply within the time stated.

Syed Saaduddin.

ꙮ

No. 259
13 September 1869

Seal
Mukhtar-ul-Mulk

Gracious Raja Sahib

Your application No. 6 written at the end of Rabi II of the current year, stating that you wish to build houses and bungalows, and lay out gardens on some land in Makthal cantonment, has been received. This would cost you thousands of rupees and the expense of future repairs would also have to be borne by you. The income of the liquor bazaar in the above cantonment is to be established. Your fixed rate village of Kothapalli badly needs repairs, which must be attended to. Hence, it is suggested that you make a *nazrana* of those houses to the Nizam, so that the construction and repairs may be taken by the Government.

ꕥ

No. 260
13 October 1869

Gracious Raja Sahib

Received a translation of the letter of Turner along with a letter of the Honourable Resident Bahadur No. 1786, dated 12 October, in regard to the passing of the army's fifty-eight horses from Bikkam and Venkatapur to Secunderabad in which it is stated that you will supply provisions to the above-mentioned people on a settled price without putting them in any trouble or hardship. No complaint in this regard should come to the Government.

ꕥ

No. 261
14 October 1869

A person named Muhammad bin Abdul Qadir, Arab *jawan* and protégé of Salam bin Ali bin Abu Bakr, *jamedar*, employed by your record keeper Raja Gajanand Pershad, who was posted at *taluq* Sugur, *sarkar* Pangal, *subah* Farkhunda Bunyad, Hyderabad, died at Wanaparthy on 7 October 1869.

ઈ

No. 262
16 October 1869

Seal

Gracious Raja Sahib

After proffering the customary greetings, it is stated that sixteen healthy bullocks are required for drawing the artillery guns. These bullocks are more easily available in Wanaparthy. Hence, you are requested to fix the price for sixteen such bullocks, and inform us here. Thereafter, the amount will be sent to you. All the other equipment required by the artillery is ready; only the bullocks are needed. As you have done in the past, you must select strong, healthy bullocks and fix reasonable prices. This will surely improve our relationship still further.

ઈ

No. 263
20 October 1869

Gracious Raja Sahib

An amount of Rs 1,000, 500 H.S. under the heads of *rusum*, other sources of revenue, and registrar of *pargana* Sugur and Kothakota for the year 1869–70 may be paid to Raghunath Rao, the clerk under Narsing Rao Humadari, agent registrar for your *ilaqa*, and a receipt may be obtained as per the rules. This is a strict Government memo.

ઈ

No. 264
26 October 1869

Greetings

Whatever you have asked Abdul Qader to convey to me orally, by that it is evident that the need for give and take is always there. In view of the same, by your willingness, it would be done. At the time of need to you and others, transactions would be made from your shop. Kindly inform the agent that at the time of meeting, he may give it in writing.

☙

No. 265
30 November 1869

In spite of comparing and finding it correct, the amount of Mirza Muhammad Beg, according to the accounts of Venkat Rao, is not submitted to the Government. Due to this, a decision about the moneylenders of the aforesaid could not be given. Hence, it is ordered by the Government that as soon as you receive this letter, the staff-holder would be sent to you to claim the amount and decide about the moneylenders. If you make excuses to pay the same, it would be referred to the *taluqdar* to call you. Hence, you must at once submit the claimed compensation, and delay in this regard will not be appreciated.

☙

No. 266
19 December 1869

Gracious Raja Sahib

From a letter written by the Major General of the Secunderabad army, and one from the Honourable Resident Bahadur, no. 2149 dated 9th of this month, which is enclosed, it is learnt that an English troop comprising three officers, 132 soldiers, seven sepoys (Indian), 411 market people along with 34 camels and 29 bullocks from Secunderabad have decamped from Secunderabad on the 16th of this present month and reached Dargah Barhane Sahib. From there, they will take the route detailed below. Therefore, it is written that in your territory, you must supply the required provisions to them, on payment of the cost. No complaint in this regard should reach the Government. If there has been any epidemic in your territory, you must inform the commanding officer of the platoon, under intimation of the Government.

Dargah Barhane Sahib
Shamshabad
Palmakul
Farooqnagar
Manakumpally/Balanagar
Jadcherla
Yudakur
Janumpet
Atakal
Kothakota
Mallepalle
Venkatapur
Bikkam
Kyatur

ജ

No. 267
1869

Gracious Raja Sahib

Orders dated 29 December (1869) of the present year asking you not to prevent the bankers and merchants from transporting the grain from your territory to Hyderabad and the cantonments of Secunderabad and Alwal were issued. Now the bankers and merchants have again submitted a petition to the Government and to the Resident Bahadur, regarding the impediments put in their way in your territory to prevent them from transporting the grain. Therefore, this is again written to remind you that the grain commands a good price during this time in the capital and the cantonments. Hence, you may not prevent the bankers and merchants from transporting the grain from your territory as you have been doing in the past. They may be allowed to bring their grain to Hyderabad and to the cantonments for sale. In this regard, you must not give them ample room for complaint against you to the

Government. You must submit a reply to both sets of order from the Government without delay.

ജ

No. 268
1869

Seal
Mukhtar-ul-Mulk

Gracious Raja Sahib

As mentioned in the notice enclosed herewith, orders addressed to you were issued on 23 December (1869) of the present year, giving permission for the merchants and bankers to bring grain in abundance to the capital, Hyderabad, and the cantonments of Chadderghat, Secunderabad and Alwal for sale. Therefore, this is to repeat that the merchants and bankers may send their grain to the capital and the cantonments as usual, and you may not prevent them from doing this. Instead, when the grain is being transported, you may write a note giving the name of the merchant, the quantity and quality of the grain, the date it is sent from there and the name of the place to which it is being transported, that is, whether to the capital or to any of the cantonments, and post it to the Government.

ജ

No. 269
1869

Seal
Mukhtar-ul-Mulk

Gracious Raja Sahib

Your letter dated 10 December (1869) of the present year with regard to the tax on salt, which is collected at the rate of rupees two per *maund* has been received. That tax on salt has nothing to do with the tax on other goods, and it has been fixed by the Government. Orders have been issued to the *ilaqadar* to collect only two rupees per heap at one time; except for the remaining revenue, road or grazing tax, no taxes may be claimed by the Banjaras and salt merchants. Therefore, in this regard included are the *taluqdar*s, *jagirdar*s and *zamindar*s. Orders stating that you must not interfere with the salt tax have already been issued to you on 23 November of this year.

ᘓ

No. 270
1869

Seal
Mukhtar-ul-Mulk

Gracious Raja Sahib

The previous orders, dated 18 October (1869) of the present year, carried instructions that you should supply provisions to a regiment coming from Bellary to Secunderabad via Raichur. Now, a letter from the Honourable Resident Bahadur has brought to our notice that a platoon of soldiers from Yadgir is also going to come to Secunderabad. It may be difficult for you to supply provisions to both; therefore, you are ordered to take precautions to ensure that you supply the required provisions to the above-mentioned regiment. There should be no room left for any complaint.

1870

No. 271
18 January 1870

Gracious Raja Sahib

From the letter of Mr. Cully Sahib, enclosed with a letter from the Honourable Resident Bahadur, No. 46 dated 14th of the present month, it has come to the knowledge of the Government that on the 8th of this month, bags containing mail from Madras were looted between Janumpet and Bhuthpur Road in your territory. Therefore, a translation of the letter that contains details about the mailbags is sent herewith. It is ordered that an immediate search be made for the thieves and the stolen bags. The robbers must be arrested and the bags recovered. The same must be reported to the Government.

ཀ

No. 272
24 January 1870

Sri Naikji Sahib

After many salutations, the Government by its favour has sent here an order in regard to depositing the amount for the partnership of a steam train to Som Raja Sahib Wanaparthy. From here, the information has been given to the aforesaid Raja Sahib. It is certain that the Naikji Sahib according to his good name and power would send an application for the partnership of the carriage at an early date. By doing this, the Government would be pleased and your status and honour would be raised much and would be a cause of great fraternity. This writing of the Naikji would be at the top of the list.

Reply of this after the consultation of Rani Sahiba may be sent immediately.

ཀ

No. 273
25 January 1870

Memo for the information of Seshgir Rao Vakil, *ilaqa* Wanaparthy.

A case has been submitted by Gori Buchi Yenkanna petitioner versus Shaikh Ahmed respondent in the department to decide the accounts of the Arabs. In this regard, Vetnapally Papiah, resident of Kesampeta of your *ilaqa*, is required to supply some information. Hence, this is to state that on the receipt of this memo, the aforesaid must be sent immediately to the department. After the enquiry, he would be sent back.

[Signed] Muhammad Abdul Qader

ജ

No. 274
1870–71

Gracious Raja Sahib

After mentioning my eagerness to see you and after all my compliments, I have to state that the month of Shaban has ended and the month of Ramzan shall start. As a follower of Islam, I have to respect and give honour to Ramzan. After Id, I shall be present before you.

Hazarat Shah Ali Shah Qadri is praying for your long life and prosperity. The *inam* that was given to him by your elders is a very old tradition and is accepted by these pious men. He has come to you for the same; thus, you being the chief, it is appropriate that the aforesaid may be given to him because he is the correct person. The things that have been given as presents to the pious people may not be stopped so as to be given to others. It is not good. In this period, if anything unusual has happened, you must forgive him by your courteousness and give him whatever it was given to him. The souls of his elders would pray for your prosperity. By way of friendship, I have written this.

Inam Jamedar

Kindly convey my best compliments to Janaki Ram and Sita Ram Pandit and the clerk.

ജ

No. 275
1870–71

Gracious Raja Sahib

Your letter has been received, along with 300 sweet tasty mangoes. They have given me much pleasure. Their sweetness is like the sweetness of sugar. You have selected and sent mangoes of the best quality. I pray that you may enjoy a long and prosperous life. Till we meet, kindly inform me now and then about your welfare.

ꕤ

No. 276
1870–71

Seal: rectangular
Raja Inderjit Bahadur
Fidvi Asaf Jah

Gracious Raja Sahib

Rai Munna Lal, who is a relative of mine, had gone to the *jatra*. As you were in Kothakota, he requested the *naib* of the village to give him a loan of Rs 100 and to send his receipt here, to me. On receiving the above-mentioned receipt, the amount was sent from here. I have sent this letter through Hukumchand and Devchand, sons of the aforesaid to the *naib*. You will receive it on your return.

ꕤ

No. 277
1870–71

Again, it is to mention that in regard to Rs 200 that was sent, it was accepted by Sahib Qibla, but the compensation of *nazrana* may be sent earlier.

ꕤ

No. 278
1870–71

Respected Janaki

In the lawsuit from the side of Sahib Qibla, an amount of Rs 100 towards *nazrana* and a fine silk shawl may be purchased and sent.

ഇ

No. 279
1870–71

High Dignity

This has become evident that Channai Deshmukhni of the *patti* mentioned above has expired. For entrusting the part of the village of the deceased mentioned above, a request along with *nazrana* has been submitted to the Government. Hence, in view of subsistence, your petition has been accorded sanction. The portion of the village of the deceased may be entrusted to him. Now, with all satisfaction, he must rehabilitate the village and the amount of the Government according to the fixed instalments may be paid annually crop-wise and the other sources of revenue, right of fees, necessaries and *watan zamindari* may be utilised by you for your expenses, and be obedient to the Government.

ഇ

No. 280
1870–71

High Dignity

It has been known from your petition dated 15th of the present that Venkat Narsing Rao, *vakil*, had taken leave through a letter written in Telugu with his signature, date and reference, and Krishna Reddi has been appointed by the Government. It has been taken notice of. According to that, the *sanad* along with the register and seal has been sent, taking the surety of the above-mentioned *vakil*. Kindly acknowledge about its receipt and the rest may be heard orally by the above-mentioned *vakil*.

ꙮ

No. 281
1870–71

Seal: rectangular
Mukhtar-ul-Mulk

Gracious Raja Sahib

It is learnt that the Rohilla thieves have taken refuge in Argi *taluq* and in Chittapur. Captain Young has been appointed to arrest them. Therefore, it is ordered that the thieves must not be given asylum or any kind of protection in your territory of Chittapur. On the contrary, you must help in their arrest.

ꙮ

No. 282
1870–71

Seal: rectangular
Mukhtar-ul-Mulk

Gracious Raja Sahib

It is learnt that in spite of the promise in your application to provide satisfactory arrangements with regard to bullock carts and drivers, complaints are being received that the carts and bullocks so far provided have been of inferior quality, causing the people much discomfort. Complaints that hire charges are being taken are also being received. This is not right. Therefore, it is ordered that two healthy bullocks, two good carts and drivers belonging to your territory who can drive the carts safely and properly must be kept ready. According to the information furnished by Sheik Daud, these carts must be provided in your territory, and no complaints should reach the Government in future.

ℵ

No. 283
1870–71

Seal: rectangular
Mukhtar-ul-Mulk

Gracious Raja Sahib

Hoover Sahib Bahadur will be travelling from here to Belgaum via Narayanpet and Bagalkot. Therefore, it is ordered that in your territory, you must supply the required provisions to him on payment. All his requests must be complied with, and he must be well-protected so that he passes safely through your territory. This is an order.

ℵ

No. 284
1870–71

Seal: rectangular
Mukhtar-ul-Mulk

Gracious Raja Sahib

The decision taken by the criminal court in the case between the petitioners, Qader Dad Khan and Azam Khan, residents of Seyri Kor'a, and the defendants, Amir Khan and Muhammad Khan, is that the defendants are to be put to death. Hence, the aforesaid *jawan*s have been arrested by the Government and are being sent to you with this order. You must take a personal interest in this matter, and send the two men to Seyri Kor'a along with an escort. After a proper announcement is made, they are to be killed and the corpses exhibited to the public for four days.

ℵ

No. 285
1870–71

Gracious Raja Sahib

According to the investigation undertaken in the case of Ram Rao and Kishan Rao, two miscreants who have absconded, it is evident that the above-mentioned people, along with some associates, escaped disguised as Bhat, Shastry, etc. They took refuge in the temples of some villages for a few days, before proceeding further. Therefore, it is ordered that wherever in your *taluq*s there is a Hindu temple or a *dharmshala*, a trusted Hindu must keep watch, and if any person arouses suspicion, you must be informed immediately. The suspected person must be kept in your custody until a complete investigation about him has been made, and only after he is proved to be harmless, may he be allowed to go. If he is not, it must be reported to the Government.

ꕤ

No. 286
1870–71

Gracious Raja Sahib

I received your letter and got the acknowledgement of the subjects. God Almighty has fixed a time for every matter; hence, those matters get completed at their own fixed time. For that, we may have patience and be content.

ꕤ

No. 287
1870–71

Raja Ram Baksh Bahadur

Dear Raja Sahib

After meeting you, I shall certainly feel happy. It is to state that your arrival at the capital would satisfy me. Hence, with all satisfaction and without any suspicion, you are to come to the capital. After you have seen the Nizam, take leave and be satisfied. The salary of the Arabs would be given after the execution of a document by you at the capital.

Nothing is to be worried.

ꕤ

No. 288
1870–71

Gracious Raja Sahib

It is learnt that the *maniwar* of Ambarpet and Chitralpally in the *pargana* of Nar'khora has been assigned to you from the beginning of the year 1852–53. You will be of help in all matters concerning the above-said villages.

[Signed] Raja Inderjit

No. 289
5 August 1871

Seal: rectangular
Mukhtar-ul-Mulk

Gracious Raja Sahib

Babu Gosayin Daheja Dhari, along with a sash, five horses for riding and loading, an armed *chaukidar* and 40 people, is travelling from the capital to the *jatra* of Sri Balaji. Therefore, you are ordered to provide two foot soldiers to accompany them and help them to cross the Krishna and Tungabhadra Rivers without difficulty. This is an order and must be complied with.

ꕤ

No. 290
1 September 1871

Gracious Raja Sahib

A summons written in Telugu with its copy and a letter from the Honourable Resident Bahadur, No. 2036 dated 31 August (1871) of the present year, sent by the Judge of the civil court, have been received and are enclosed. Therefore, it is ordered that the signature of Gulab Khan, a resident of Wanaparthy, be obtained on the reverse of the summons and it must be returned to the Government within twenty days. The copy may be given to the aforesaid, and he must be instructed to present himself there on 15 September.

ꕥ

No. 291
1871

Seal: round

From: Secretary Government Railway Department
To: Sawai Raja Ram Krishna Rao Balwant Bahiri Bahadur

Subject:

In reply to the *ilaqa* letter No. 1 dated 6 December 1871, received on 25 December of the same year, along with two *hundi*s amounting to Rs 33,300 Halli Sicca, from the shop of Ram Chander moneylender towards the share money of the railway line running from Gulbarga to Hyderabad from the total money of Rs 1,00,000 mentioned in the application in *hundi*s through the Secretary of the office and submitted in the Government treasury, are received.

[Signed] Ganpath Rao
Secretary Government, Railway Department

ꕥ

No. 292
1871–72

Dear Brother

After saluting you and longing to know your welfare, it is to state that two applications mentioned about sending the amount of daily allowance and the other claiming some mango trees and twelve fish are received. I learnt the affairs mentioned in it. Before this, it is evident from the application of Syed Shah Mansoor that at present the trees are not ready. After I received your application, I have ordered the grafting of the trees. If God may help, those shall be ready in two months. In sending the amount, some objections have come. The reason is that the implementer is sick. After two months, the amount and the trees both would be sent. The season of grapes is continuing; you may kindly inform how many grapes have been harvested. I hope at present you might have one or two grapevines. Kindly send them to me.

ꕤ

No. 293
1871–72

High Dignity Janaki

Your letter is received and I came to know the affairs through Nagamma that all commodities and goods of past and present have been seen by Begum Sahiba. In the future, you may be satisfied. The *nazrana* and pension Rs 2,000 and Rs 1,000 are due. You may accept *nazrana* on your responsibility. The amount of *taluq* Sugur through Mama Nahi may be submitted within eight days. Otherwise, you shall be guilty to the Government. Begum Sahiba requires four decanters and one valuable sari. You may buy it and send it urgently. Further, it is to state that Sadullah Khan is posted as *tehsildar* Sugur by transferring Qadir Ali Khan. This order is sent to the *taluq* on 25 February (1873) and the aforesaid has come and is working.

The dues of the previous *nazrana*, an amount of Rs 3,000, have been received from the shop of Dalab Rao.

ꕤ

No. 294
1871–72

Requisition for *khadi* made; hence, it is ordered to send 200 *khadi*. Yet, only eighty *khadi* have been received; the remaining 120 may be prepared urgently and sent quickly.

ꕥ

No. 295
1871–72

Seal: rectangular
Suroor Afza Begum

Your Excellency

According to your letter, Mama Tahniyal Asil is being sent to you. You must compare the things, and all matters must be discussed in the presence of Qadir Ali Khan. Then you may present yourself here.

ꕥ

No. 296
1871–72

Gracious Raja Sahib

A notice written in Telugu and its copy, along with a letter from the Honourable Resident Bahadur and a stamp of 14 *annas*, sent by the Judge, Kurnool, have been received and are enclosed. Therefore, it is ordered that the signature of Purka Yellaiah, a resident of Ramkishtapur, be taken on the reverse of the notice, which must be returned to the Government. The copy may be given to him.

ꕥ

No. 297
1871–72

Gracious Raja Sahib

Evidently you have taken over the responsibility of paying off the loan given to the late Elchi Rao, employed with Raja Ram Baksh. Hence, this is to state that the people from the aforesaid Raja's *ilaqa* will be coming to you for settlement of their dues. Therefore, you must decide about the above-mentioned loan and pay it off without delay. No complaints in this regard should come to the Government.

ꙮ

No. 298
1871–72

Gracious Raja Sahib

The Resident Bahadur has enquired about any epidemics prevalent in the area between Bellary and Secunderabad. Therefore, this is to state that the required information may be sent immediately.

ꙮ

No. 299
1871–72

Gracious Raja Sahib

Orders were issued earlier regarding the payment of the compensation of *maghruta* to the accountant of village Cholpally and, secondly, not to claim *rusum* for the open land of Balanagar and Gangapur and the other villages belonging to Umdat-ud-Daulah Bahadur. However, you have not yet sent the *mal-e-maghruta* and are still claiming the *rusum* for the open Banjara land. This is wrong on your part. Therefore, this is to state that *mal-e-maghruta* may be given to the aforesaid accountant immediately and you may not claim the *rusum* for the open Banjara land. This is a strict Government memo.

ꙮ

No. 300
1871–72

Gracious Raja Sahib

Due to the purchase of additional grain, there is now a sufficient supply in the markets of the capital, and the cantonments of Secunderabad and Alwal. Therefore, this is to state that on receipt of this order, you may stop purchasing grain. The Government may be informed regarding the quantity and quality of whatever has already been purchased. If any merchant desires to take back his grain, it may be returned to him, but no complaints in this regard should reach the Government. Arrangements may be made to transport the grain already purchased at the fixed price to the capital.

❧

No. 301
1871–72

Seal: rectangular
Raja Chandu Lal Bahadur

Gracious Raja Sahib

The compensation of other sources of revenue, *rusum* and portion of necessaries of *zamindar*s of *pargana* Avancha, village Doloor as is usual by the concern of Taju Khan may be sent so that the payment of the Government amount through the *zamindar*s may be made.

❧

No. 302
1871–72

To Lakmi Das and Laxmi Das

Your letter with your brother and an order of the Government is received, and I came to know about the subject matter. In respect of payment of interest towards the amount of salary, the prepared list made me joyful. In every suit, this friend trusts the patronage. Hence, based on this, why have you shortened the beginnings of the letter although this friend has power and authority? As you have said, it is compulsory for a friend to complete it. The Raja is our friend from a previous time. I could have brought the order by myself and appeared before the Nawab Sahib and narrated my affairs. However, since some days, I am not well. I have a high temperature; Azam Khan *taluqdar* knows it well. Moreover, Kishan Rao, who is appointed *taluqdar* at *pargana* Sugur, etc., went to see him. It is my misfortune that I developed more illness. Hence, for my treatment, I went to Dr. Rogers at Kurnool. By the favour of God, I recovered and I thought of appearing to tell all my affairs. Hence, I have written in detail to the Nawab Sahib, who has gladly accepted it. In case this friend would become healthy once more, he would personally appear. I have also sent Venkata Naik some days before in your service. He shall tell you in detail about me. In respect of the interest of the amount, your friend is trustworthy; you may mention it. In the Government hospital, Moore by name is the doctor for distributing medicines. I hope that you shall take the permission of the Nawab Sahib and send it to the doctor because the doctor is about to leave for foreign land.

ℵ

No. 303
1871–72

By the voice of unseen, the most divine.
Seal: rectangular
Raja Ram Baksh Bahadur

Gracious Raja Sahib

The petition sent by the Collector made me happy. It has come out from the Royal Court as I desired. In other words, the omen has come out according to the desire of my conscience and made me happy. By seeing this omen, I felt excessively happy. The Almighty has helped me. You have fortitude from good old days, which cannot be erased. May Allah help me. After receiving the honour of whatever I could do for you, I shall not withhold it. You may also bless me so that you may succeed in your aim.

ℵ

No. 304
1871–72

Respectable Courteous Raja Sahib

After much humility, I have to state that I presented myself before you along with Syed Kalinullah Khan to state my conditions of life. However, as some people were present there, I did not see proper to say anything before them; hence, I came away. On that day when Sri Abdul Qader came, I told him all my miseries. After hearing it and seeing all my documents, he promised to tell before you if you would ask him. Kind sir, I have nobody except you in this vast world to help me; thus, I request you to help me.

Petitioner, Muhammad Amin Uz Zaman.

ꟸ

No. 305
1871–72

To Azam Khan *taluqdar, pargana* Sugur

One letter written by Simha, agent, is received and I came to know about the affairs. An application of Sawai Raja Sahib is enclosed herewith. After the study of the same, you may help him as a friend and in all other suits you may send them to the Government by your recommendation.

ꟸ

No. 306
1871–72

Dear Sharfu Miyan

After formal salutation and eagerness to know your health by Makhdum Sahib, it is to state that all is well here, and I hope that you might be also well. The other thing is what you have said for the contract of the skins. Hence, the details of the rate of purchase and other things of the application may kindly be written and sent through Qadir Sahib so that I may be satisfied. For this reason only, I have sent Qadir Sahib to you to know all the details. In addition, I have to go to Bombay, but for this reason, I have postponed it to find out what steps are to be taken in this regard and where to approach. Hence, I have not gone to Bombay. Therefore, writing all the details, you send it through Qadir Sahib. You said that I must apply in January; thus, I have written to you. No sooner than you see this letter, write a reply to it and send it. I am eagerly awaiting the reply. Your letter may be delivered to Makdum Sahib in Bada Bazaar, Secunderabad.

ꙮ

No. 307
1871–72

Request application of Raja Rameshwar Rao states that *watan zamindari*, *patti* Gopalpet, is his ancestral right since long before. Hence, orders were issued to arrest Syed Hussain and to present him. In lieu of that, *sanad* of Gopalpet was to be issued, after which this humble servant informed that he would submit a *nazrana* of Rs 50,000 for *sanad* and *khilat*. The Government has not entertained it. Now I am waiting for your benevolence and generosity that you would order to sanction *sanad* and *khilat* to this obedient servant for which I am submitting Rs 75,000 *nazrana* in the Government. This obedient servant would be satisfied and obedient in a released position.

ꙮ

No. 308
1871–72

To the revenue collectors and *jagirdar*s, etc.

From the application of Sawai Raja Rameshwar Rao Bahadur, it is evident that Srimati Kesai, *deshmukhni*, *patti* Gopalpet, etc., *pargana* Haveli, *sarkar* above-cited had deviated from her early promises and had an intention of adopting a son. Hence, after enquiry, according to the condition of the issued *sanad*, she is entitled for these rights for her life till she is mentally fit, but she has no rights to adopt a son. Hence, the aforesaid Raja may take possession of the above, and this would be hereditary to him. This is a strict order in this regard to be complied with.

1872

No. 309
12 May 1872

Seal: round
Niyabad-e-Diwani 1219
Nizam-ul-Mulk
Asaf Jah Bahadur

To the *taluqdar*s, *naib*s, *jagirdar*s, *zamindar*s, headmen, accountants, etc., of the Nizam's Dominions.

Sawai Raja Ram Krishna Rao Balwant Bahiri Bahadur will be travelling from the capital Farkhunda Bunyad, Hyderabad to the *jatra* of Balaji. He will be accompanied by twenty-five armed horsemen, seventy foot soldiers and four peons. Four stages will be covered by palanquin, and five in a carriage. Ten ponies suitable for riding will also be with the group. It is therefore written that provisions may be purchased by him on the way on payment of the cost price, and he must not misuse his power. This is an order and must be complied with.

[Written in English] On this being presented, the concerned British authority is requested to give the bearer a licence to carry arms while travelling in British territory should the need arise.

[Signed] Assistant Resident

ꕤ

No. 310
12 June 1872

Memo of the Police Office

Sri Ram Singh, resident of Residency, went to Kurnool for some purchases. There he bought betel leaves. While returning, he died at village Janumpet, which is the Government *ilaqa*. At his death, his clothes and utensils that were with him were kept in custody of the village headman and accountant of the village. A sister and wife of the deceased are present who have submitted an application for giving away the clothes and utensils of the deceased to them. In case the above-cited goods are demanded by the Government, it should be sent. As per rules, after the goods are claimed by the Government, a notice is to be pasted for the heirs to appear within six months. In addition, after the period is over and there is no claim, then the same is to be distributed among the *jawans*. While sending the goods, the signatures of the village headman and accountant on the list are essential. Hence, this memorandum is sent to the Resident so that after seeing it, he may kindly let this office know whether the same may be sent through the Government, with the list signed by the village headman and accountant.

ᘓ

No. 311
14 June 1872

Gracious Raja Sahib

A letter from the police station with regard to the demise of Sri Ram Singh, a resident of Janumpet, has been received. I mention that before starting on his journey from Kurnool, his clothes and belongings were left with the headmen of the village. The legal heirs of the dead person have now submitted a petition asking for the same. With regard to this letter, a letter from the Honourable Resident Bahadur No. 1371 dated 13 June of the current year has also been received. A copy of the above is enclosed. Therefore, it is written that a list of the articles belonging to the late Ram Singh may be obtained and sent to the Government, duly signed by the headman and accountant of his village.

ᘓ

No. 312
9 July 1872

Letter from the office of the Secretary Government Railway.

Checked and found correct, Syed Kalimuddin Mir Munshi.

As per the orders of the Government Minister in reply to two memorandums of Govind Venkoba, *naib*, No. 1 and 2 dated 7 and 8 July 1872, along with two *hundis* amounting to Rs 33,400 H.S. to complete the figure of Rs 1,00,000 in response to the application of Raja Ram Krishna Rao Balwant Bahiri Deshmukh, *samasthan* Wanaparthy, in regard to shares of railway expenses running from Gulbarga to Hyderabad, it is to inform you that the above-mentioned *hundis* are submitted in the Government treasury through the Secretary of your office, for a period of a fortnight, for the payments. Hence, after the period is over and those are cashed and submitted in the Government treasury, it would be taken into accounts.

[Signed] Ganpath Rao Sri Kishan

ཨ

No. 313
9 July 1872

Letter from the office of the Secretary Government Railway.

Checked and found correct, Syed Kalimuddin Mir Munshi.

As per the orders of the Government Minister, two memorandums of Govind Venkoba Naik, No. 1 and 2 dated 7 and 8 July 1872, along with two *hundis* of Rs. 10,400 H.S. towards Rs 1,00,000 as stated in the application of Raja Ram Krishna Rao Balwant Bahiri Bahadur Deshmukh, *samasthan* Wanaparthy, in respect of share money of the railways running from Gulbarga to Hyderabad, it is to state that the *hundis* mentioned above have been credited in the Government treasury through the Secretary of this office but as the period of encashment of the mentioned above *hundis* is mentioned fifteen days hence, after the expiry of the date, the amount submitted in the above-cited treasury would be taken into accounts.

[Signed] Ganpath Rao Sri Kishan

ꕥ

No. 314
11 December 1872

Gracious Raja Sahib

The Honourable Resident Bahadur has sent information over the wireless that on the 8th of this month, a box containing a golden deity was stolen from the Raja of Travancore. Therefore, you are ordered to take a personal interest in conducting a search for it, and if it is recovered, it must be reported at once.

ꕥ

No. 315
30 December 1872

Gracious Raja Sahib

This is in reply to your letter No. 4 dated 16 December of the present year, containing the information that the search for the stolen box from the Maharaja Sahib of Travancore has been successful. This is to state that since the box has been recovered, it is no longer necessary to search for it.

ꕥ

No. 316
1872

Seal: rectangular
Mukhtar-ul-Mulk

Gracious Raja Sahib

From the letter of the Honourable Resident Bahadur, it is learnt that the Royal Artillery is starting on the march from Nirmal to Secunderabad on 15 September (1872) of the present year. Therefore, it is ordered that before the arrival of the regiment in your territory, all the shops selling liquor must be closed; no spirits or alcoholic beverages should be sold to the soldiers. This is an order and must be complied with.

ꕤ

No. 317
1872

Seal: rectangular
Mukhtar-ul-Mulk

Gracious Raja Sahib

From a letter of the Honourable Resident Bahadur, it is learnt that the 26th platoon, numbering 705 sepoys and 2,100 people of the bazaar, along with 570 bullocks and 35 horses, will reach Adoni on 22 October (1872) of the present year via Secunderabad, and from there, will go on to Kyatur. Therefore, it is ordered that upon the arrival of the platoon at Janumpet, Yudakur, Atakal, Kothakota, Venkatapur and Bikkam, according to the enclosed letter, you may kindly supply provision to them. No complaint should reach the Government in this regard. And in someone else's territory, where it is not possible for you to do this, you must appoint a farmer to supply them with the above-mentioned provisions. This is an order and must be complied with.

1873

No. 318
16 January 1873

Gracious Raja Sahib

From the memorandum of the Assistant Superintendent Sahib of Electricity and a letter from the Honourable Resident Bahadur, No. 69

dated 10 of the current month and year, it is evident that the aforesaid Sahib will visit Chadderghat this month, in connection with the electricity. He will come via Venkatapur, making three halts on the way. He will inform you four days before his arrival. Therefore, it is ordered that upon his arrival in your estate, a carriage may be given to him on payment of a reasonable hire charge. This may be taken as an official letter from the Prime Minister. You are strictly enjoined to obey these orders.

ꕤ

No. 319
22 January 1873

Gracious Raja Sahib

From the letter of the Honourable Resident Bahadur, No. 469 dated 22nd of the present month, it is learnt that a troop of thirty horses will reach Raichur on the 21st of the above-mentioned month. From there, they will come to Secunderabad. Therefore, it is written that wherever they halt in your territory you must supply 135 *seers* *gram* or *kulthi*, 30 *kattas* of green grass and twenty-five iron pegs on payment of the cost price. See that no complaint in this regard reaches the Government.

1874–1875

No. 320
1875

Translation of the memo of the Military Secretary addressed to Major Louis dated 3 December 1875 AD. For the information of the Resident, a letter No. 5730 of the Secretary to the Government of Madras, dated 22nd of the previous month, in regard to the decamping of the Company from Madras is ordered. Hence, a Company from Secunderabad shall be reduced.

1876–1883

No. 321
1882–83

Submitted before High Dignity

It is to state that I am suffering from a particular tumour called *naru*, and information has come from my home that my mother is also severely ill and facing economic difficulties. Therefore, I request you to most humbly sanction the payment of this month's salary and the salary of the other month of both these brothers. For this only I have come to you. You are my feeder.

Applicant, Muhammad Yousuf, Mir Shikari.

1884

No. 322
1 January 1884

To the Highly Elevated Nizam, Honourable Sir

Since olden days, from the office of Raja Rayan Bahadur Amanath Vanth, the *zamindar*s of *samasthan* Gadwal, Sugur, Jatprole and Amarchinta, and the office that is Shiv Rah Bahadur and *samasthan* Shorapur and Gurgunta have been made permanent. Hence, it is prayed that the aforesaid *zamindar*s according to the orders of His Exalted Highness would attend the procession of coronation as in routine. Kindly order for it.

Seshgir Rao, *vakil*, *samasthan* Wanaparthy.

No. 323
16 January 1884

Gracious Raja Sahib

The coronation ceremony of the Nizam is to be held next month. Hence, this is to state that by the end of this month, you are required to present yourself at the Nizam's palace.

ꙮ

No. 324
18 January 1884

Receipt submitted on behalf of Sawai Raja Rameshwar Rao Balwant Bahiri Bahadur, *samasthan* Wanaparthy, while residing in the capital.

One elephant with a canopy.
One elephant with a litter.

Submitted by Seshgir Rao, *vakil, samasthan* Wanaparthy.

ꙮ

No. 325
21 January 1884

From the chief feudatory to His Highness

On the 7th of the coming month, a ceremony of coronation of His Exalted Highness has to be held. Therefore, this is to state that at the end of this month, you should appear before the Nizam.

ꙮ

No. 326
1884

[On Nizam's Government letterhead] You must be present on 6 February 1884, Tuesday, at the Durbar of His Highness in *khilat* at 9 a.m.

ထ

No. 327
10 February 1884

To His Exalted Highness

During this period, under the order of the Government and invitation to attend the procession of coronation of your Exalted Highness, this is to humbly submit that when all the Rajas and *zamindar*s of the state come there and I will come there to submit my humble *nazrana*, I do not know how some of the Rajas would behave because they neither know the old traditions nor the dignity of the rank. If they would not behave according to the old customs, there would develop a difference, and the Government employees do not like it and they do not wish for it. Although the Government employees know it well, the honour bestowed upon them is by the Nizam. This old servant has many favours; thus it is humbly submitted that Lord Governor General has said, the copy of those are enclosed herewith. What the late king at his journey to Bombay had bestowed had also been written. After all, the wish of this old slave is that at the time of distributing robes of honour, whatever has been fixed for must not be exceeded and may not underestimate others' rank. Kindly honour me by an immediate reply.

ထ

No. 328
25 February 1884

List of gifts sent by Nawab Shuja-ud-Daulah Salar Jung Bahadur to Sawai Raja Rameshwar Rao Balwant Bahiri Bahadur, *zamindar* of Wanaparthy.

Masala for *pandan*, 5 *kani*.
Anwarkal, one.

Bottles of scent, two.
Gram dal, 12 *seers*, one tray.
Toor dal, 12 *seers*, one tray.
Sugar, 15 *seers*, two trays.
Sugar candy, 14 *seers*, two trays.
Ghee, 22 *seers*.
Butter, 8 *seers*.
Meat, 9 *seers*.
Cash, Rs 150 H.S.

ꙮ

No. 329
3 November 1884

To the Honourable Ruler

For the last 100 years, the Government has posted Arabs at *samasthan* Wanaparthy. This is only to let the ryots know that the Government is sovereign over the *samasthan* and that the *samasthan* owes allegiance to the Government. Secondly, among all the *zamindars*, the *zamindar* of the above-mentioned *samasthan* may be proud that the Government has shown its favour by the presence of the Arabs. Hence, in consideration of the above reason, the Government has honoured the *samasthan*. So the late minister also continued this record. As the stationery is deducted from the *peshkash*, so the salary of the troops is also adjusted in it. In this regard, a report has come from the *samasthan* that the first *taluqdar*, Nagarkurnool, has sent two letters, No. 376 and 386, in reply to letter No. 1125 from the office of the Nazim-e-jamiat and No. 1393 from the office of the Military Secretary to recall the Arabs from Wanaparthy and send them to the first *taluqdar*. Respected Sir, this is an honour given by the Government from a long time ago. Thus, if abolished now, the *samasthan* will be dishonoured among the *zamindars*. The Government is all-powerful and can honour the *samasthan*. Hence, I most humbly request your honour to issue an order to the Military Secretary, asking him to write to the district *taluqdar* to send back the Arabs and to post them at Wanaparthy as before.

Applicant, Seshgir Rao, *vakil*, *samasthan* Wanaparthy.

ꙮ

No. 330
1884–85

The description of the horse that has been stolen away in Alwal from Alam Ali Khan: a fat dun-coloured horse; a fold at the forehead; no beard; the upper and lower lips inclined towards white; and shallow on stomach at heel. On the right hand side, at the latter part of the rider's leg and at the hoof a line—a big white spot. At the whipping leg above the heel: bay colour. The white hoofs of both the legs and feet are netted. Age 5 years.

No. 331
1884–85

Dear Uncle

After salutation, it is to state that in reply to my letter, you have given the report of the ill health of my brother Sarandaz Khan. Now, it has also been conveyed that he is better. After receiving this letter, you send my brother to me because all the people in my house and the people of Barhane Sahib are remembering him much.

No. 332
9 May 1885

The translation [in Urdu from English] of a memorandum from the magistrate, Secunderabad, addressed to Major Acess Sahib Bahadur.

This is to inform you that Subrat Rao, a sepoy, *ilaqa* belonging to the 8th Company, 16th platoon of Secunderabad, has gone on leave. It is alleged that he has stolen ornaments and cash, the details of which are listed below, from the house of Venkat Swami, *havaldar*, *ilaqa* 32nd platoon.

Hence, it is ordered that if he is found in the capital, he may be arrested. Total value of the articles: Rs 174.

One gold neck ornament, called a *gotam pusalu*, weight about 5 *tola*s. Rs 100.
One gold neck ornament called a *gluco*, weight 1 ½ *tola*s. Rs 15.
One gold ornament called a *jambu*, weight 1 *tola*. Rs. 16
One gold ring, weight ¼ *tola*. Rs 5
One embroidered Madras kerchief. Rs 7
One silk kerchief. Rs 1
Cash. Rs 30.

It is said that the aforesaid sepoy went towards Ellora where he has relatives. A physical description of the sepoy is enclosed herewith. Physical description of Subrat Rao, a sepoy belonging to *ilaqa* 16th platoon: height 5 feet 7 inches, dark complexion, age 25 years. He was last seen on Sunday 7 May 1865 in Secunderabad.

No. 333
12 May 1885

True Copy.
Copy of the order with the seal of Nawab Mukhtar-ul-Mulk, to Laxma Reddi, *deshmukh* of Nar'khora, dated 23 August 1867.

[On the side] This copy is given on the application of Venkata Chari, the *vakil* of *samasthan* Wanaparthy, on 12 May 1885.

The Hali Sicca is being enforced in all the districts of the dominion of Hyderabad. Therefore, it is ordered that from the beginning of the year 1866–67, the right of fees and district revenue must be paid in Hali Sicca by the people of the *taluq*s under Raja Ram Krishna Rao Bahiri Balwant Bahadur, son of the late Raja Rameshwar Rao.

No. 334
14 October 1885

Gracious Raja Sahib

Warmest greetings and eagerness to see you. This is to state that the family of Narshima Chary of Avancha has been getting an allowance of Rs 180 annually for several years. In 1883–84, it was given to him through Ananth Ram, *naib* of Kesampeta. Now, the *naib* has told the aforesaid Narsimha Chary to get the payment for 1884–85 from the *samasthan* and has written an application to the Raja Sahib in this regard. However, because of his youth, Narshima Chary does not know how to get there. Hence, you are requested to pay this sum of Rs 180 for the year 1884–85 to Krishna Chary Velgonda, who has brought you this letter. That would certainly please me.

ൽ

No. 335
1885–86

Application to Nawab Salar Jung Bahadur. Previously when I submitted an application for assigning the hereditary rights of Ashapur and releasing a *sanad* for it, it was agreed. Yet, till now, no orders about this have been received by Azam Khan *taluqdar*. Hence, again, I request that this slave may be honoured by a *sanad* and an order in this regard may be sent to the aforesaid *taluqdar*.

1886

No. 336
5 February 1886

Seal: rectangular
Mir Laiq Ali Khan, Muneer-ud-daula Bahadur.

Gracious Raja Sahib

After perusing your letter No. 2 dated 26 April 1885, it is stated that the people who killed the criminal Miyan Sahib deserve a reward. Mir Zulfiqar Ali, a Government Officer, has written that the criminal was fired at and shot dead by a group of police constables, whose names are furnished below. This had been reported to this office. Therefore, the disbursement of a reward Rs 300 was agreed upon by *samasthan* Wanaparthy. The statement of disbursement is being prepared and sent. In reply to your request, a letter is enclosed to this effect, and the above-mentioned amount is being sent with the foot soldiers. The constables may be directed to go and collect the reward from the above-mentioned officer.

Copy.
Letter from the office of Syed Mir Zulfiqar Ali, former Regional Superintendent of Police, dated 3 February 1886.

The required information has been sent to this office through an official letter No. 537 dated 16 January (1886) of the year mentioned above. The details regarding the deserving people among whom the reward of Rs 300 H.S. given by *samasthan* Wanaparthy are to be distributed are as follows. I sent a group of police constables with a head constable to search in all directions for Miyan Sahib and to arrest him. Finally, the men listed below found and attacked him in a forest. Ramji, an informer who has only one hand, pointed out Miyan Sahib and gave information to the police. Therefore, it would be appropriate to give Ramji a silver staff worth Rs 20, and Rs 40 each may be paid to the other members of the group.

Raja Ram, police head constable.
Abdur Rahman, police constable I.
Abdual Ghani, police constable II.
Chandraiah, constable.
Venkataiah, constable.
Balaiah, constable.
Sheshaiah, constable.
Ramji, a Lambada informer.

[Signed] Zulfiqar Ali

ഇ

No. 337
19 September 1886

Seal: rectangular
Turab Ali Khan

To the *taluqdar*s, *naib*s of present and future and *deshmukhs*, *deshpande*s, headmen and accountants, etc., *taluq* Borgal, *sarkar* Lovil.

It had been written that our *khas jagir*, village Mallepally, *taluq* above-mentioned, *sarkar* above-cited, *subah* aforesaid, on the application of Raja Rameshwar Rao Balwant Bahiri Bahadur *samasthan* Wanaparthy is leased out to him under the fixed rate amount of Rs 1,500 H.S. annually from the beginning of the year 1886–87 under all heads including goods; remaining revenues; liquor tax; butcher's tax; village artisan tax; date tree tax; mango tree tax; tamarind tax; sugar tax; tree tax; right of procession; right of metal working; streams, wells, tanks and flowing rivulets; *kotwa*s, etc., of populated and unpopulated areas of lime stone, metals, other sources of revenue, and *rusumdar*s had already been appointed. Now, the aforesaid fixed rate holder may be deemed permanent in every aspect, and he may be helped accordingly. For him, the amount of revenue tax may not be claimed in excess. This is a strict order that may be complied with without any hesitation. This copy may be provided to the aforesaid fixed rate holder.

Turab Ali Khan.

ജ

No. 338
1886

Draft of request application to Nawab Salar Jung Bahadur.

In reply to your kind letter, this is to state that Narsiah has been present in the Government office since eight days. Due to my absence, much delay is caused in several cases to the Government. By the treatment of Dr. Maclean, I am better now. The amount of the first instalment of the present year 1885–86 is submitted to Kishan Rao, *taluqdar*. Without waiting for further orders, in consultation with the said *taluqdar*, I received a letter on 4 September of the present year (1886); I have no power to disobey you, and in the past, I had paid homage to you. I have submitted an order to the Government, and I was waiting to appear personally. However, unfortunately, I fell ill, and due to acute fever, I suffered so much, it was not possible for me to sit or get up. I could not mention the trouble caused by it. I admitted myself to the doctor of Kurnool, who gave me medicines, but I was not cured; hence I called on him again, but his medicines did not cure me. I confined myself to my home. I desire your favour and permission to go to the doctor who is treating me carefully. You could also know it by his report. In some matters, the Government is competent, which is sufficient. In view of the details, you may pass orders, and I shall carry it out without any excuse and hesitation. The amount of stipulated fixed rate revenue of the previous year was submitted in consultation with Lakshmi Das Seth. For the present year also, it shall be submitted through the aforesaid Seth as routine to the Government according to the fixed instalment. Hence, I request you to pass orders asking Maknaji not to insist on and demand the same.

No. 339
15 February 1887

Copy.
To the sacred superior punishable authority.

Taluq Gopalpet was previously in the *ilaqa samasthan* Wanaparthy. Gopal Rao Bahiri Balwant Bahadur Raja of *samasthan* Wanaparthy, *taluq* above-cited, due to relations that he had with Venkat Reddi, son of Ranga Reddi, and being of the same ancestors, gave it to him on the condition that he may keep it with him till he had his own issues to continue the line and he shall not be entitled to retain it if any one successor died issueless and Gopalpet shall again be restored to *samasthan* Wanaparthy, and he shall not have a right to adopt any son. Smt. Laxmi Narsai, *deshmukhni* of Gopalpet, died issueless. In spite of two such orders of the Government, issued by Raja Chandu Lal Bahadur and the other by the late Prime Minister of the state, which prohibit adoption of a son, the copies of which are also enclosed herewith, the clerks of that place are in favour of adopting a son. Hence, this suit under the legal guidance of Mr. Norton, bar-at-law, has been submitted in the Government, and the same is under investigation of Mr. Dunlop, Inspector General of Revenue. The aforesaid officer at present is on Government tour to districts. Hence, I expect from your exalted employees that till the investigation of the case is complete, the village Gopalpet may be taken under Government custody in consultation with the *taluqdar* Nagarkurnool including the agent of this *samasthan*; otherwise the clerks of the aforesaid *deshmukni* would appropriate the money and funds. After the enquiry is over and the reality of this *samasthan* is traced out, the village of the above-mentioned *taluq* may be included in the villages of *samasthan* Wanaparthy and a *sanad* and robes of honour may be sanctioned to the Raja Sahib of *samasthan* Wanaparthy so that the right person may not be neglected. May God bring prosperity to you and to your descendants.

Slave Seshgir Rao, *vakil*,
samasthan Wanaparthy.

༄

No. 340
January/February 1887

To His Exalted Highness

My Lord, Gopalpet in the days of Sawai Venkat Reddi Raja of *samasthan* Wanaparthy was given to Ranga Reddi due to a close relationship and being of the same ancestors and family on the condition that they could take benefit out of it till they could continue their line with successors, and in case, there comes a break by having no issues, they must not adopt a son and must return Gopalpet to [Wanaparthy] *samasthan* because it has been obtained from *samasthan* Wanaparthy. Since then, it was with Laxmi Narsai, *deshmukhni* Gopalpet. The aforesaid *deshmukhni* died issueless, and no person of her side is alive now. Hence, I request my Lord that according to the condition mentioned above, the village Gopalpet is a right of *samasthan* Wanaparthy. Therefore, it may be included in *samasthan* Wanaparthy and a *sanad* and robes of honour may be sanctioned to Raja Rameshwar Rao, Raja of *samasthan* Wanaparthy, so that the person concerned may not be deprived of his rights. A *nazrana* for the village above according to my conditions is now submitted.

Applicant Seshgir Rao, *vakil*,
samasthan Wanaparthy.

No. 341
1887–88

Gracious Raja Sahib

After expressing in the formal way my salutation and eagerness to see you, I hope that the people of both the sides might be healthy. Previously your courteous letter was received, which gave me much pleasure; though it was a short one, it was reassuring. It has erased the feeling of hate from the hearts of us, and if God wills it, it shall not happen in the future. Now as per the old traditions, we must strengthen our relations, at least by freely sending letters about our welfare.

1888–1890

No. 342
1889–90

High Dignity

The clerks of Raja Rameshwar Rao have agreed upon and submitted it in the Government that the destruction of *patti* Rachala has occurred. According to the witness of Tum Ramchander Reddi, *deshmukh*, and Gangu Ram Krishna Reddi, *deshmukh pargana* Ghanapur, if they confess it, they must repay the loss without any excuse. Therefore, this case was put up before the *panchayat*. During the investigation, whatever proof is put against them from Rameshwar Rao, it should be preserved, deeming it as advantageous by those above-mentioned people so that they may be satisfied.

1911

No. 343

Delhi Durbar

Sums total taken for the expenditure by gracious Sri Raja Sahib while going to Delhi Durbar in the month of November 1911

100	From the main treasury
	800
	200
	1,000
50	Given by the Raja Sahib of Gadwal for the servants (Halli currency)
50	Brought by Raja Sahib of Wanaparthy while going to Delhi
30	Taken from Raja Sahib for the bestowal on the servant of Gadwal, in absence of Seshagiri Rao
199-3-0	Given by Sankumaddi Ramanna for the purpose of train fares
72	Given by Sankumaddi Ramanna for train fares at Wadi
12	Given to Brahmins at the time of religious rites at Prayag
6-15-6	To Brahmins for meals at Prayag
2-12-0	Given by Ramanna at Kasi for a brass pot
1000	Given by Gracious Sri Ammayyagaru for train fares
	100 once
	900 once
	1,000
100	Taken from Raja Sahib
	50 at Calcutta
	50 at Ayodhya
	100
200	Given by Rani Sahiba for train fares at Lucknow
100	Rani Sahiba for train fares at Agra

100	Taken for expense through Kashanna at Delhi, while going to 'Kurukshetram'
16	Given by Kasanna at Delhi
1400	Purchase of clothes at Kasi given by Rani Sahiba to pay Kashinath
15-8-0	Received through Sankumaddi Ramanna on account of shortage to purchase clothes at Delhi
5	Received through Ramanna for the arrangement of carts to go to the Railway Station
500	Given by Rani Sahiba for train fares, while returning from Delhi
120	Given by Rani Sahiba for train fares at Ujjaini
5	Given by Ramanna at Khandwa, on account of shortage to purchase a sovereign 15 10 — 5

5520-6-6
(10-0-0 Given under the account at Calcutta)
5530-6-6